Janice VanCleave's
SOLAR SYSTEM

Spectacular Science Projects

Janice VanCleave's
Solar System

Mind-Boggling Experiments You Can Turn into Science Fair Projects

John Wiley & Sons, Inc.
New York • Chichester • Weinheim • Brisbane • Singapore • Toronto

Published by John Wiley & Sons, Inc.
Published simultaneously in Canada

Design and production by Navta Associates, Inc.

The publisher and the author have made every reasonable effort to ensure that the experiments and activities in this book are safe when conducted as instructed but assume no responsibility for any damage caused or sustained while performing the experiments or activities in this book. Parents, guardians, and/or teachers should supervise young readers who undertake the experiments and activities in this book.

Library of Congress Cataloging-in-Publication Data
VanCleave, Janice Pratt.
   [Solar system]
   Janice VanCleave's solar system : mind-boggling experiments you
can turn into science fair projects.
     p. cm. — (Spectacular science projects)
   Includes index.
   Summary: Provides instructions for a variety of experiments
and science fair projects exploring the solar system, including the sun,
moon, planets, comets, and meteorites.
   ISBN 0-471-32204-0 (pbk. : alk. paper)
   1. Solar system—Experiments Juvenile literature. 2. Science
projects Juvenile literature. [1. Solar system—Experiments.
2. Experiments. 3. Science projects.] I. Title. Title: Solar
system. III. Series: VanCleave, Janice Pratt. Janice VanCleave's
spectacular science projects.
QB501.3.V36 2000
523.2'078—dc21
                                            99–15479

Printed in the United States of America
10 9 8 7 6 5 4 3 2

CONTENTS

DEDICATION

It is a pleasure to dedicate this book to Dr. Glenn S. Orton. Glenn is a Senior Research Scientist at the Jet Propulsion Laboratory of the California Institute of Technology. An astronomer and space scientist who specializes in investigating the structure and composition of planetary atmospheres, he is best known for his research on Jupiter and Saturn. I have learned a great deal about astronomy from Glenn and enjoyed exchanging ideas with him about modeling astronomy experiments. One of the most exciting things that I've learned about astronomy is that there is so much more to learn.

ACKNOWLEDGMENTS

I wish to express my appreciation to a group of science specialists for their valuable assistance in providing information or assisting me in finding it: members of the Central Texas Astronomical Society, including Paul Derrick, Johnny Barton, and John W. McAnally. All proudly profess to be active amateur astronomers. Paul is the author of the "Stargazer" column in the *Waco* (Tex.) *Tribune-Herald*. Johnny is an officer of the club. John is on the staff of the Association of Lunar and Planetary Observers, where he is acting Assistant Coordinator for Transit Timings, Jupiter Section.

E. Robert Fanick is a chemist at Southwest Research Institute in San Antonio, Texas, and Virginia Malone is a science assessment consultant. These two very special people have provided a great deal of valuable information, which has made this book even more understandable and fun.

A special note of gratitude to these educators, who assisted by pretesting the activities and/or by providing scientific information: Holly Harris, China Spring Intermediate School, China Spring, Texas; Laura Roberts, St. Matthews Elementary School, Louisville, Kentucky; James Roberts, Oldham County High School, Buckner, Kentucky; and Anne Skrabanek, Perry, Texas.

Introduction

Science is a search for answers. Science projects are good ways to learn more about science as you search for the answers to specific problems. This book will give you guidance and provide ideas, but you must do your part in the search by planning experiments, finding and recording information related to the problem, and organizing the data collected to find the answer to the problem. Sharing your findings by presenting your project at science fairs will be a rewarding experience if you have properly prepared for the exhibit. Trying to assemble a project overnight results in frustration, and you cheat yourself out of the fun of being a science detective. Solving a scientific mystery, like solving a detective mystery, requires planning and careful collecting of facts. The following sections provide suggestions for how to get started on this scientific quest. Start the project with curiosity and a desire to learn something new.

SELECT A TOPIC

The 20 chapters in this book focus on specific topics and suggest many possible problems to solve. Each topic has one "cookbook" experiment—follow the recipe and the result is guaranteed. Approximate metric equivalents have been given along with English measurements. Try several or all of these easy experiments before choosing the topic you like best and want to know more about. Regardless of the problem you choose to solve, what you discover will make you more knowledgeable about the solar system.

KEEP A JOURNAL

Purchase a bound notebook in which you will write everything relating to the project. This is your journal. It will contain your original ideas as well as ideas you get from books or from people like teachers and scientists. It will include descriptions of your experiments as well as diagrams, photographs, and written observations of all your results. Every entry should be as neat as possible and dated. Information from your journal can be used to write a report of your project, and you will want to display the journal with your completed project. A neat, orderly journal provides a complete and accurate record of your project from start to finish. It is also proof of the time you spent sleuthing out the answers to the scientific mystery you undertook to solve.

LET'S EXPLORE

This section of each chapter follows the sample experiment and provides additional questions about the problem presented in the experiment. By making small changes to some part of the sample experiment, you achieve new results. Think about why these new results might have happened.

SHOW TIME!

This section goes a step further than "Let's Explore" by offering more ideas for problems to solve and questions to answer related to the general topic of the chapter. You can use the format of the sample experiment to design your own experiments to solve the questions asked in "Let's Explore" and "Show Time!" Your own experiment should follow the sample experiment's format and include a single question about one idea, a list of necessary materials, a detailed step-by-step procedure, written results with diagrams, graphs, and charts if they seem helpful, and a conclusion answering and explaining the question. Include any information you found through research to clarify your answer. When you design your own experiments, make sure to get adult approval if supplies or procedures other than those given in this book are used.

If you want to make a science fair project, study the information listed here and after each sample experiment in the book to develop your ideas into a real science fair exhibit. Use the suggestions that best apply to the project topic you have chosen. Keep in mind that while your display represents all the work you have done, it must tell the story of the project in such a way that it attracts and holds the interest of the viewer. So keep it simple. Do not try to cram all of your information into one place. To have more space on the display and still exhibit all your work, keep some of the charts, graphs, pictures, and other materials in your journal instead of on the display board itself.

The actual size and shape of displays will vary, depending on local science fair officials, so you will have to check the rules for your science fair. Most exhibits are allowed to be 48 inches (122 cm) wide, 30 inches (76 cm) deep, and 108 inches (274 cm) high. These are maximum measurements, and your display may be smaller. A three-sided backboard, as shown here, is usually the best way to display your work. Wooden panels can be hinged together, but you can also use sturdy cardboard pieces taped together to form a very inexpensive but presentable exhibit.

A good title of about 6 to 10 words should be placed at the top of the center

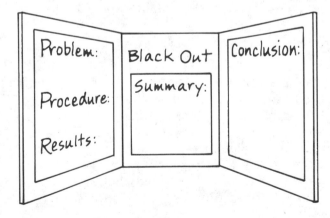

panel. The title should capture the theme of the project but should not be the same as the problem statements. For example, if the problem under question is *What causes a solar eclipse?* a good title of the project may be "Black Out." The title and other headings should be neat and large enough to be readable at a distance of about 3 feet (1 m). You can glue letters to the backboard (use precut letters that you buy or letters that you cut out of construction paper), or you can stencil the letters for all the titles. Add a short summary paragraph of about 100 words directly under the title to explain the scientific principles involved. A person who has no knowledge of the topic should be able to easily understand the basic idea of the project just from reading the summary. Have friends read the summary and ask for their reactions. Did they understand the project? It is up to you to clarify any points that need explaining.

There are no set rules about the position of the information on the display. However, it all needs to be well organized, with the title and summary paragraph as the main point at the top of the center panel, and the remaining material placed neatly from left to right under specific headings. Choices of headings will depend on how you wish to display the information. Separate headings for Problem, Procedure, Results, and Conclusion may be used.

The judges give points for how clearly you are able to discuss the project and explain its purpose, procedure, results, and conclusion. The display should be organized so that it explains everything, but your ability to discuss your project and answer the judges' questions convinces them that you did the work and understand what you have done. Practice a speech in front of friends, and invite them to ask you questions. If you do not know the answer to a question, never guess or make up an answer or just say, "I don't know." Instead, you can say that you did not discover that answer during your research and then offer other information that you found of interest about the project. Be proud of the project and approach the judges with enthusiasm about your work.

CHECK IT OUT!

Read about your topic in many books and magazines. You are more likely to have a successful project if you are well informed about the topic. For the topics in this book, some tips are provided about specific places to look for information. Record in your journal all the information you find, and include for each source the author's name, the book title (or magazine name and article title), the page number, where it was published, the publisher's name, and the year of publication.

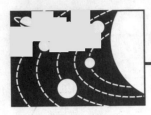

1

Line Up

PROBLEM

What did people in the past think the universe looked like?

Materials

yardstick (meterstick)
22-by-28-inch (55-by-70-cm) piece of
   poster board
pencil
26-inch (65-cm) piece of string
school glue
2-inch (5-cm) Styrofoam craft balls
   (available at craft stores)
marking pen

Procedure

1. Lay the yardstick (meterstick) across the middle of the poster board, parallel with the long sides.

2. Using the pencil, make nine small dots on the poster board next to the yard-stick, one every 3 inches (7.5 cm) from the end. The last dot will be 1 inch (2.5 cm) from the edge of the poster board.

3. Tie a loop in one end of the string.

4. Place the pencil point through the loop and stand the point on the second dot from the left side of the poster board. Pull the string outward to stretch it over the first dot. Hold the string on the first dot with your thumb as you move the pencil point across the poster board to draw the largest part of a circle.

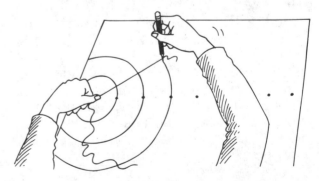

5. Repeat step 4 for each of the remaining dots.

6. Glue one Styrofoam ball to each of the first eight dots.

7. Using the marking pen, add labels as shown, and draw stars in the space beyond Saturn.

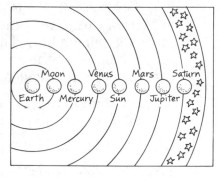

Results

You have made a model that shows how people in the past thought the universe was organized.

Why?

In this experiment, a **geocentric** (Earth-centered) model of the **universe** (Earth and all other natural objects in outer space) is made. This model was proposed by the ancient astronomer Ptolemy, who lived and worked in Alexandria, Greece, in the second century A.D. Ptolemy believed that Earth was motionless and that the Moon, the planets, and the Sun **revolved** (moved around a center point) around Earth. An outer dome of stars was thought to exist beyond the farthest planet (then thought to be Saturn). Ptolemy believed that in relation to their starry background, the Sun and the Moon continued to move along their paths around Earth, while other **celestial bodies** (natural objects in the sky) seemed to wander. These wandering celestial bodies were called planets, from the Greek word for wanderers. Today's model of the Sun and its **planets** (celestial bodies that move in a path around a sun) is **heliocentric** (sun-centered) with nine planets.

LET'S EXPLORE

Nicolaus Copernicus (1473–1543), a Polish astronomer, proposed a heliocentric model of the universe. In Copernicus's model, the celestial bodies were in the following order from the central, stationary Sun: Mercury, Venus, Earth with the Moon as a **satellite** (a body revolving around another body), Mars, Jupiter, and Saturn. Use the same materials as in the previous experiment to show Copernicus's model of the universe.

SHOW TIME!

1. The first models of the universe were mainly models of our solar system. A **solar system** is a group of celestial bodies that **orbit** (move in a curved path around) a star called a **sun.** A modern model of our solar system shows Earth as one of the nine known planets that revolve around the Sun. Make a drawing that depicts the modern concept of the solar system.

2. The average distance between Earth and the Sun is 93 million miles (149 million km). This distance is called an **astronomical unit** (AU) and is used as a measure of distance in the solar system. The AU distance for any planet can be calculated by dividing the planet's average distance in miles (km) by 93 million miles (149 million km). For example, the average distance of Mercury from the Sun is 36 million miles (58 million km). Thus, the AU distance between the Sun and Mercury can be calculated as follows:

   36 million miles ÷ 93 million miles = 0.4 AU
   58 million km   ÷ 149 million km = 0.4 AU

Mercury is 0.4 AU from the Sun.

Prepare a table similar to the one shown here, giving the average distances of

Average Distances of Planets from the Sun		
Planet	**Millions of Miles (Millions of km)**	**Astronomical Units (AU)**
Mercury	36 (58)	0.4
Venus		
Earth		
Mars		
Jupiter		
Saturn		
Uranus		
Neptune		
Pluto		

the planets in whole millions of miles (km) from the Sun (see the appendix) and the AU distances calculated to the nearest decimal place, as in the previous example.

3. Use the AU distances to make a scale model of the distances of the planets from the Sun. A **scale model** is a model made in proportion to the object or objects that it represents. For example, a scale of 1 cm : 1 AU means that 1 cm on the model represents 1 AU.

Using the scale of 1 cm : 1 AU, draw a line 39.7 cm long on a paper to represent 39.7 AU, the distance between the Sun and Pluto, the outermost known planet in our solar system. Place a small circle with rays at the left end of the line to represent the Sun and a dot at the opposite end for the planet Pluto. Using the AU distances of each planet, place a dot on this line for each planet according to the scale. Label each planet.

CHECK IT OUT!

When Copernicus proposed a heliocentric model of the universe, it was not widely accepted. About 70 years after Copernicus's death, Galileo Galilei (1564–1642), an Italian astronomer and physicist, used a telescope he made to study the heavens. His observations supported Copernicus's heliocentric idea. Find out more about Galileo's observations. Were Galileo's ideas about the universe accepted?

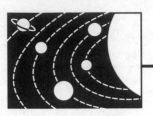
Opposite

PROBLEM

How does Earth appear to move as seen from space above the North Pole (Earth's most northern point)?

Materials

paper plate
black marker
sharpened pencil
adult helper

Procedure

1. With the plate facedown, use the marker to label the right edge of the plate E for east and the opposite edge W for west.

2. Label the area near the center of the plate North Pole. Draw a curved arrow along the bottom edge of the plate.

3. Ask your adult helper to insert the point of the pencil through the center of the plate so the point exits the North Pole area.

4. Hold the pencil so that you are looking at the North Pole side of the plate. Rotate the pencil so the plate turns in the direction of the arrow (west to east). Note the direction, clockwise or counterclockwise, that the plate turns.

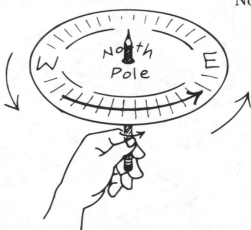

Results

The plate turns in a counterclockwise direction.

Why?

The plate, like Earth, rotates west to east. Rotate means that it turns on its **axis** (an imaginary north-to-south line through the center of a celestial body). As seen from above the **North Pole,** the most northern point on Earth and the north end of Earth's axis, Earth rotates counterclockwise.

LET'S EXPLORE

How does Earth appear to move as seen from space above the **South Pole** (most southern point on Earth and the south end of Earth's axis)? Use the plate from the experiment. Remove the pencil and turn the plate over so that the E (east) label is under the right side. Label the edges E and W as before. Label the area near the center as South Pole. Draw the arrow along the top edge of the plate. The arrows on either side of the plate will be in line with each other. Insert the pencil through the center of the plate as before. Hold the pencil so that the North

Pole side of the plate faces up. Rotate the pencil so that the plate turns in the direction of the arrow (west to east). Again, note the counterclockwise direction that the plate turns. While rotating the pencil, raise the plate over your head so that you are looking at the South Pole side. Note that the plate continues to rotate in the west-to-east direction, but when you are looking at the South Pole, the rotation is clockwise.

SHOW TIME!

1. Why do stars appear to change position as Earth moves? Shape a walnut-size piece of clay into a ball, then gently hit one side of the ball against a flat surface several times to flatten the side. Stop when you have what looks like half a ball. The clay half-ball is a model of the **Northern Hemisphere,** which is the region north of Earth's **equator** (imaginary line perpendicular to the axis that divides a celestial body in half). Place a 12-by-12-inch (30-by-30-cm) piece of white poster board on a table and set the Earth model in the center of the poster board. Stick a paper clip in the side of the clay as shown to represent an observer from

Earth. Randomly stick 8 to 10 stick-on stars on the inside surface of the bowl. The bowl is half of a **celestial globe,** which is a model of an imaginary sphere around Earth called the **celestial sphere.** Stick a strip of masking tape around the outside rim of the bowl. The tape represents the celestial sphere's equator. Label two small pieces of tape, one E and the other W. Stick the pieces of tape on opposite sides of the bowl. Position the bowl over the Earth model on the poster board so the model is centered under the bowl with the paper clip pointing toward the W (west) label on the bowl. Lift the bowl just enough so that your helper can rotate the poster board counterclockwise one half turn. As the Earth model turns, note the west-to-east path that the paper clip traces through the stars and the apparent east-to-west path of the stars.

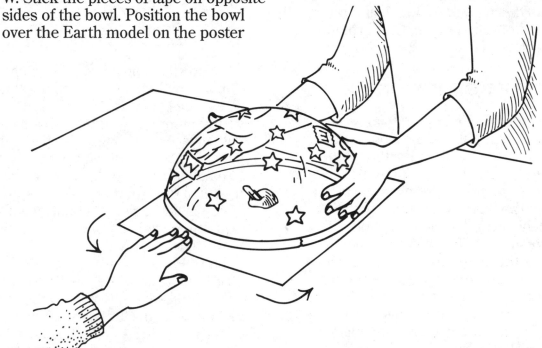

2. Make the part of a celestial globe around **Polaris** (the North Star, which is the star closest to the point above Earth's North Pole). Do this using an umbrella with eight sections (preferably a solid, dark color) for one hemisphere and stick-on stars to represent the stars of different **constellations** (groups of stars that appear to make patterns in the sky). Set the umbrella on a table and rotate the umbrella by turning the handle slowly in a counterclockwise direction. Continue until one complete rotation has been made. As you turn the umbrella, observe the position of the constellations in relation to one another, to Polaris, and to the tabletop. (The tabletop represents the **horizon,** an imaginary line where the sky seems to meet Earth.) Since the stars stay above the horizon, they are said to be circumpolar. For more information about the rotation of Earth and **circumpolar stars,** see pages 45–55 in *Janice VanCleave's Constellations for Every Kid* (New York: Wiley, 1997).

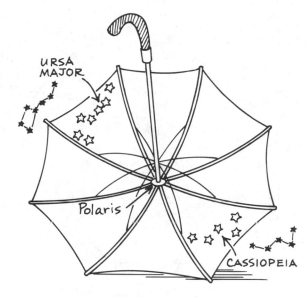

CHECK IT OUT!

Latitude and longitude are *coordinates* (numbers that mark the location of a place) used on a *terrestrial globe* (model of Earth). In a similar way, declination and right ascension are coordinates used on a celestial globe. Find out more about how these coordinates work. For information, see pages 14–24 in *Janice VanCleave's Constellations for Every Kid* (New York: Wiley, 1997).

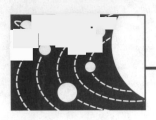

3

Bong!

PROBLEM

How do astronomers use vibrations to determine the nature of the Sun's interior?

Materials

stemmed water glass
tap water
metal spoon

Procedure

1. Fill the glass about three-fourths full with water.

2. Gently tap the side of the glass with the spoon. As you listen to the sound, observe the surface of the water.

Results

When a sound is produced, the water has tiny waves on its surface.

Why?

Tapping the glass makes the glass and its contents **vibrate** (move quickly back and forth). The back-and-forth motion of the glass pushes on the water inside the glass, causing waves to form on the water's surface. The motion also causes movement in the air outside the glass, which causes sound waves to travel through the air to your ears.

One back-and-forth motion is called a vibration, and the number of vibrations in a specific time period is called **frequency**. **Astronomers** (scientists who study celestial bodies) use vibrations to study the interior of the Sun. Vibrations pass from the Sun's interior to its gaseous surface, causing it to move up and down.

While the frequency of the vibrations produced by striking the glass is many vibrations in 1 second, the frequency of some solar sounds is only 1 vibration in 5 minutes. You are able to see the waves on the water and hear the sound produced by the vibrating glass. But computers are needed to distinguish between the vibrations produced by the Sun. The study of the interior of the Sun by observing how its surface vibrates is called **helioseismology.**

LET'S EXPLORE

By observing the different vibrations that occur on the Sun's surface, astronomers can determine different things about the Sun, such as its motion, temperature, pressure, composition, and the density of its inner layers. **Density** is a measure of the amount of **mass** (measure of the amount of matter in an object) in a specific **volume** (space occupied by a three-dimensional object).

Demonstrate how the density of a **fluid** (gas or liquid) affects the frequency of its vibrations by repeating the experiment using glasses filled with liquids of increasing density, such as water (least dense), cooking oil, and ketchup (most dense). It may be easier to detect a difference in sound than a difference in the number of waves on the surface of the liquids.

SHOW TIME!

1. Prepare a display of the structure of the Sun's layers similar to the one shown here. Add a legend providing information about the different layers. For information about the Sun's

layers, see pages 95–96 in Dinah Moche's *Astronomy* (New York: Wiley, 1996).

LAYERS OF THE SUN

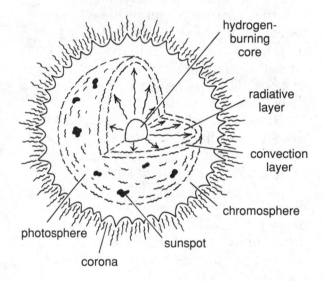

2a. Look for **sunspots** (cool, dark spots on the Sun's surface) on a projected image of the Sun. *CAUTION: Never look directly at the Sun. It can permanently damage your eyes or blind you.* It is safe to study the Sun's surface by using binoculars or a telescope to project the Sun's image onto a paper screen. Without looking through the instrument, point it at the Sun, and then focus the image of the Sun on a sheet of white poster board. Design a way to secure the instrument and poster board so that they do not move. This will allow you to draw the image and mark the sunspots. One way is to secure the poster board to a tree or building and use a tripod to hold the telescope. If binoculars are used, position them on a stool. *NOTE: Ask an adult to make sure the lenses of the instrument are clean.*

The Sun's image will be easier to see if you cut a hole in a second piece of poster board, 12 inches (30 cm) square. The hole should be large enough to fit around the front (Sun-facing) telescope lens or one of the binoculars' front lenses. Insert the lens of the instrument through the hole. This sheet of poster board casts a shadow on the poster board screen behind the telescope, which will make it easier to see the Sun's image.

Tape a sheet of tracing paper to the poster board screen. Trace the Sun's image on the paper and mark any sunspots. You may have to make observations for several days before you see any sunspots. As you observe the Sun's image, note that it moves to one side of your drawing as Earth rotates. For more information about sunspots and another method of viewing them, see pages 94–95 in Heather Couper and Nigel Henbest's *How the Universe Works* (Pleasantville, NY: Reader's Digest Association, 1994).

2b. Repeat the previous experiment over several days. Compare the drawings to determine in which direction the sunspots move. What causes sunspots? How big are sunspots? Are sunspots permanent? For information, see pages 60–61 in Ann-Jeanette Campbell's *Amazing Space* (New York: Wiley, 1997).

CHECK IT OUT!

The surface of the Sun is not smooth, but bumpy, because of the movement of the many gases that make up the Sun. The bumps on its surface are called *granules* and are the tops of rising currents of hot gases. How large are granules? How long do they last? What are supergranules? For information, see pages 101–102 in Dinah Moche's *Astronomy* (New York: Wiley, 1996).

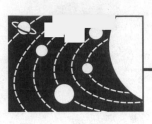

4

Moon Mapping

PROBLEM

What changes, if any, occur in the Moon's apparent shape from day to day?

Materials

calendar with times of moonrise and
    moonset (if available)
drawing compass
ruler
5 sheets of typing paper
pencil
clipboard

Procedure

1. Prior to starting your Moon observations, study a calendar with the times of **moonrise** (when the Moon rises above the eastern horizon) and **moonset** (when the Moon sets or sinks below the western horizon) for the 29 dates of your observation. (The horizon is an imaginary line where the sky seems to meet Earth.) If a calendar is not available, use the table below to determine approximately when the Moon will rise and set each day. The

Approximate Times of Moonrise and Moonset			
Shape	Phase of the Moon	Moonrise	Moonset
●	New	Dawn	Sunset
◐	First Quarter	Noon	Midnight
○	Full	Sunset	Dawn
◑	Third Quarter	Midnight	Noon

times on the table vary during different seasons of the year. Newspapers and television weather reports are also a source of moonrise and moonset times.

2. Use the compass and ruler to draw six circles with 3-inch (7.5-cm) diameters on 4 of the sheets of paper and five circles on the last sheet. Each circle will represent the Moon.

3. Date the circles, starting with the date of day 1 and ending with the date of day 29.

4. On day 1, observe the Moon and use the pencil to shade the portion of the first circle on the paper to represent the portion of the Moon that is not lighted by the Sun and therefore not visible. *NOTE: Make no observation for at least 3 days before and after new moon—when the side of the Moon facing Earth is dark. The new moon is close to the Sun and you could damage your eyes if you look at it.*

5. Repeat steps 3 and 4 each day for as many days as possible. If the weather docs not pcrmit, or you are unable to make an observation for another reason, leave the circles for those dates empty.

6. On day 29, after all the drawings are completed, study them to determine if the Moon's apparent shape changed from day to day.

Results

The apparent shape of the Moon changed from day to day. The changes are called **phases of the Moon** or **Moon phases.**

Why?

Generally half of the Moon is lighted by the Sun, but to observers on Earth, all of the lighted side is not always visible.

The relative position of the Sun and the Moon changes daily. The farther the Moon is from the Sun in the Moon's orbit around Earth, the more of the lighted side we see. When the Moon is opposite the Sun with Earth in between, the lighted side faces the Earth. This is called **full moon**. When the Moon is between Earth and the Sun, the lighted side faces away from the Earth. This is called **new moon**.

The rotation of Earth on its axis causes the Sun and the Moon generally to rise in the east and set in the west. But while the time of sunrise varies by only about 1 minute each day, moonrise is about 50 minutes later each day. This delay in moonrise is due to the eastward rotation of the Moon around the Earth. The new moon rises with the Sun. But the next day, the Moon rises about 50 minutes after the Sun rises. The day after that, it rises 50 minutes later, and so on. About 1 week after new moon, the **first quarter moon** rises at noon. About 2 weeks after new moon, the full moon rises at sunset, and about 3 weeks after new moon, the **third quarter moon** rises at midnight. Finally, about 29 days after new moon, the new moon again rises at sunrise.

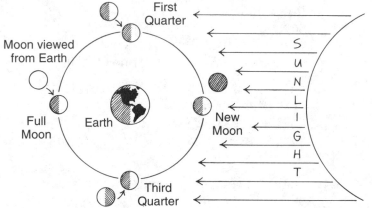

LET'S EXPLORE

1. Do the surface features of the Moon change from day to day? Repeat the experiment using binoculars or a low-power telescope. Study the appearance of the Moon and shade the daily drawings to indicate any dark regions in the lighted area of the Moon. Note that the view of the Moon through a telescope is inverted (upside down), whereas the view with your naked eye or binoculars is not inverted.

2. For the days that you did not observe the Moon during the original experiment, use the data collected to guess what the Moon's shape would have been on those days. For information

about the shapes and names of the Moon's surface features, see pages 332–351 in Jay M. Pasachoff and Donald H. Menzel's *A Field Guide to Stars and Planets* (Boston: Houghton Mifflin, 1992). **Science Fair Hint:** Use the drawings as part of your display to show the phases of the Moon and the Moon's surface features.

SHOW TIME!

Model the phases of the Moon by shaping a walnut-size piece of dark-colored modeling clay into a ball to represent the Moon. Stick the ball on the point of a pencil. In a darkened room, ask a helper to hold a flashlight so that the light shines toward your face. The flashlight represents the Sun and you are Earth. Holding the pencil in your hand, place the Moon model midway between you and the light. This shows the position of Earth, the Moon, and the Sun during new moon. Use an astronomy book to find out more information about the positions of Earth, Moon, and the Sun during the different phases of the Moon. Have another helper take photos of you showing the different positions for each phase. Use the photos to prepare a display.

CHECK IT OUT!

When the visible portion of the lighted side of the Moon increases, the Moon is said to *wax*, and when the visible portion of the lighted side decreases, it is said to *wane*. Find out more about the waxing and waning of the Moon. What are the names of the phases between the new moon, first quarter moon, full moon, and third quarter moon? For information about phases of the Moon, see page 40 in Dinah L. Moche's *Astronomy Today* (New York: Random House, 1995).

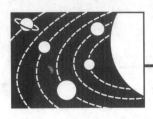

5

Shadows

PROBLEM

How can the Moon cover the Sun?

Materials

grape-size ball of modeling clay
2 sharpened pencils
3-inch (7.5-cm) Styrofoam ball

Procedure

1. Place the ball of clay on the point of one of the pencils and the Styrofoam ball on the other pencil's point.

2. Hold the pencil with the Styrofoam ball at arm's length in your left hand so that the ball is in front of your face.

3. Close one eye and hold the pencil with the clay ball in your right hand so that the ball is in front of but not touching your open eye. Slowly move the clay ball away from your face toward the Styrofoam ball. As you move the clay ball, observe how much of the Styrofoam ball is hidden by the clay ball at different distances.

Results

The closer the clay ball is to your face, the more it hides the Styrofoam ball.

Why?

The closer an object is to your eye, the bigger is its **apparent size** (the size an object at a distance appears to be). The small ball of clay can totally cover the larger Styrofoam ball, blocking it from view. In the same way, the Moon, with a diameter of 2,173 miles (3,476 km), can sometimes cover the much larger Sun, which has a diameter of 870,000 miles (1,392,000 km).

When the Moon passes directly between the Sun and Earth, and all three are in a straight line, the Moon **eclipses** (passes in front of and blocks the light of) the Sun. In this position, observers on Earth see a **solar eclipse.** The Sun is about 400 times larger than the Moon, but at times during the Moon's **ellipse** (oval) -shaped orbit, the Moon is about 400 times nearer Earth. It is in this position that the Moon and Sun appear to be the same size. In a solar eclipse in which the Moon appears as large as the Sun, the Moon completely covers the Sun. This event is called a **total solar eclipse.**

LET'S EXPLORE

When the Moon is far enough from Earth to appear smaller than the Sun, the Moon does not completely eclipse the Sun. An outer ring of the Sun's **photosphere** (bright visible surface of the Sun) is visible. This event is called an **annular eclipse.** Demonstrate an annular eclipse by repeating the experiment, slowly moving the clay ball away from your face until only a small outer ring of the Styrofoam ball is visible around the clay ball. **Science Fair Hint:** Make drawings to represent the Sun during the different types of solar eclipse.

SHOW TIME!

1. Like all shadows, the Moon's shadow consists of a dark inner region called the **umbra** and a lighter outer region called the **penumbra.** Observe these parts of a shadow by positioning a desk lamp as high as possible above a sheet of paper on the desk. Hold your hand under the lamp about 1 inch (2.5 cm) above the paper. Observe the inner and outer parts of your hand's shadow.

2a. During a solar eclipse, only part of Earth is in the shadow of the Moon. Observers in the umbra see a total solar eclipse, while those in the penumbra see a **partial solar eclipse,** in which only part of the Sun is blocked by the Moon. Observers outside the Moon's shadow see no eclipse. Design a poster of a solar eclipse, similar to the one shown here, to show why a solar eclipse is not seen by all observers on the daytime side of Earth.

2b. During an annular eclipse, the umbra of the Moon's shadow does not reach Earth. Add a diagram to the poster designed in the previous experiment to represent an annular eclipse.

3. Never look at the Sun with your naked eye, even during an eclipse. One way to safely view an eclipse is by looking at a projected image of the Sun. For information about this method, see chapter 3, "Bong!"

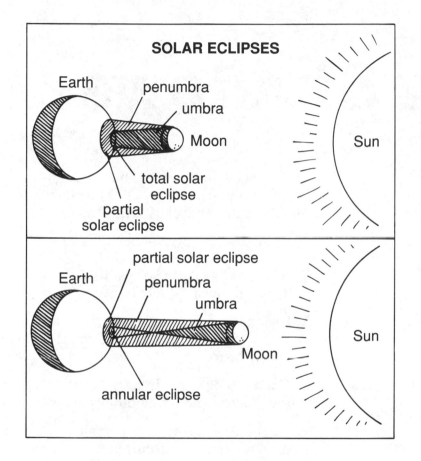

SOLAR ECLIPSES

Earth — penumbra — umbra — Moon — Sun — total solar eclipse — partial solar eclipse

Earth — partial solar eclipse — penumbra — umbra — Moon — Sun — annular eclipse

CHECK IT OUT!

Because Earth rotates, during a total solar eclipse the small umbra of the Moon's shadow sweeps across Earth's surface. Since the umbra is only about 167 miles (269 km) wide, a total eclipse of the Sun occurs rarely in any one spot on Earth. Scientists can predict the location of future solar eclipses. For information about the dates and sites of future eclipses, see Philip S. Harrington's *Eclipse!* (New York: Wiley, 1997).

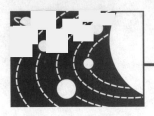

6

Earth Shadows

PROBLEM

How does the Moon move through Earth's shadow?

Materials

2 sharpened pencils
3-inch (7.5-cm) Styrofoam ball
modeling clay
ruler
flashlight
3 or 4 books
drawing compass
3-inch (7.5-cm) square of white poster
 paper
scissors

Procedure

1. Insert about 1 inch (2.5 cm) of the pointed end of one pencil in the Styrofoam ball. Use the clay to stand the pencil on the floor about 12 inches (30 cm) in front of a wall. The pencil should be vertical with the ball on top.

2. Place the flashlight about 18 inches (45 cm) from the ball. Use the books to raise the flashlight so that its light is directed toward the ball.

3. Use the compass and ruler to draw a 2-inch (5-cm)-diameter circle on the poster board.

4. Cut out the paper circle and tape it to the pointed end of the other pencil.

5. Hold the pencil so that the paper circle is about 2 inches (5 cm) in front of the wall and to the left of the ball's shadow on the wall.

6. Slowly move the paper circle to the left so that it passes completely through the ball's shadow.

7. Observe the shape of the ball's shadow on the paper circle as the paper circle moves through the shadow.

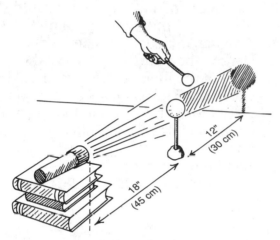

Results

First, only part of the paper circle is covered by the ball's shadow. Then all of the circle is covered. Eventually, the circle moves completely out of the shadow.

Why?

In this model, the flashlight (the Sun), the ball (Earth), and the paper circle (the Moon) are in line with each other. When this happens, the shadow of the ball falls on the paper circle, much like Earth's shadow falls on the Moon in an event called a **lunar eclipse** (the movement of the Moon into Earth's shadow). Like the model, when the Moon, Earth, and the Sun are in a straight line with Earth in the middle, the entire Moon moves into the shadow of Earth. This event is called a **total lunar eclipse.**

LET'S EXPLORE

The Moon's orbit in relation to Earth's is tilted about 5°. Thus, during the Moon's monthly revolution around Earth, it does not usually pass into Earth's shadow at full moon. Because of this, a lunar eclipse does not occur every month. In some eclipses, only part of the Moon passes into Earth's shadow, thus producing a **partial lunar eclipse.** Show the movement of the Moon without an eclipse by moving the paper circle so that it is above or below the shadow of the ball. Then repeat the experiment, moving the paper circle so that only about half of it moves through the ball's shadow as in a partial lunar eclipse. **Science Fair Hint:** Make sequence drawings of the paper circle as it moves to represent the results of each experiment. Label the different events Total Eclipse, No Eclipse, and Partial Eclipse.

SHOW TIME!

1. During a total lunar eclipse, the Moon can take on a reddish tint. This is caused by red light **refracted** (bent) by Earth's **atmosphere** (the blanket of gas surrounding a celestial body). **White light,** which is visible light such as that from the Sun or a flashlight, is made up of all the different colors of the **spectrum** (a band of colored lights produced when visible light is separated): red, orange, yellow, green, blue, indigo, and violet. The Moon's reddish color is produced by dust particles in Earth's atmosphere, which scatters the rays of most colors of visible light, but allows red light to pass through.

Demonstrate how particles in dishwashing liquid can scatter some colors of light but allow others to pass through. Fill a 10-ounce (300-ml) clear plastic glass with water and place the glass on a table about 6 inches (15 cm) in front of a white paper screen taped to a wall. Place a flashlight about 6 inches (15 cm) from the glass on the side opposite the screen. Use 2 or more books to raise the flashlight so that the light shines through the middle of the water and onto the screen. Add 1 teaspoon (5 ml) of milky-colored dishwashing liquid to the water and stir. Darken the room and observe the color of the light on the screen. Add 1 teaspoon (5 ml) of dishwashing liquid three more times, noting the color of the light after each addition.

For more information about the red color of the Moon during

a total lunar eclipse, see page 45 in Heather Couper and Nigel Henbest's *How the Universe Works* (Pleasantville, NY: Reader's Digest Association, 1994).

2. Lunar eclipses only occur when the Moon is full. Design a poster of a total lunar eclipse, similar to the one here, to show why a total lunar eclipse is seen by all observers on the nighttime side of Earth.

CHECK IT OUT!

During a total lunar eclipse, how long does it take for the Moon to be totally covered by Earth's shadow? What is the general time required for a complete lunar eclipse? For information, see pages 108–109 in Jay M. Pasachoff's *Peterson First Guides: Astronomy* (Boston: Houghton Mifflin, 1988).

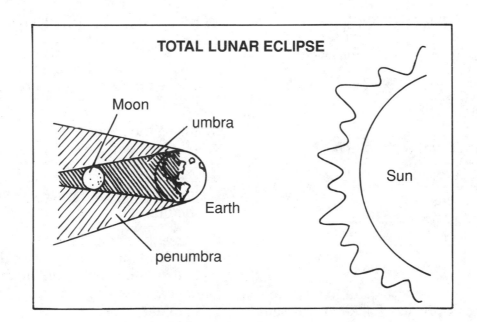

TOTAL LUNAR ECLIPSE

Moon

umbra

Earth

penumbra

Sun

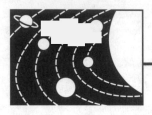

7

Around and Around

PROBLEM

What is the shape of a planet's orbit?

Materials

black pen
ruler
10-inch (25-cm) square of poster
  board
sharpened pencil
2 paper brads
8-inch (20-cm) piece of string
adult helper

Procedure

1. Use the pen to mark a dot in the center of the poster board. Label the dot Sun and draw rays around the dot. Mark a second dot 2 inches (2.5 cm) away from the first dot.

2. Ask an adult to use the pencil to make a hole through each dot on the poster board.

3. Insert the paper brads in the holes and secure them.

4. Tie the ends of the string together to form a loop, then place the loop around the brads.

5. Place the point of the pen against the inside of the loop, and with the string taut and the pen's point against the paper, move the pen around inside the loop until it is back at the starting point.

Results

An oval shape is drawn.

Why?

The oval shape drawn is an ellipse, which is the shape of the orbit of a planet.

While a circle has one center point, an ellipse has two **foci** (points in line with each other and on either side of the center point of the ellipse), represented by the two brads. For each planet's orbit, the Sun is located at one focus, and nothing is at the other focus.

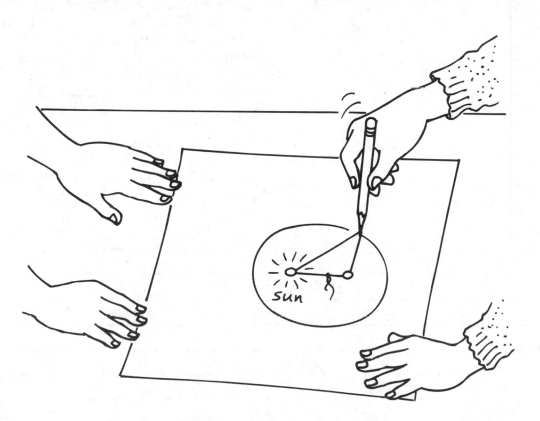

On a planet's orbit, the point closest to the Sun is called the **perihelion** and the point farthest from the Sun is called the **aphelion**. (In the figure the orbit shown is more elongated than are any of the planets' orbits.)

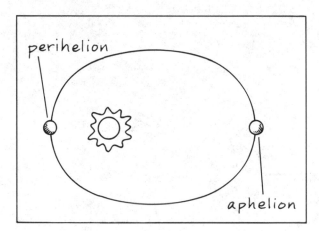

LET'S EXPLORE

How does the **focal distance** (the distance between the foci) of an ellipse affect its shape? Repeat the previous experiment three times. First, leave the brads where they are and draw the ellipse with a red pen. Second, place the second brad 1 inch (2.5 cm) away from the first brad and use a blue pen to trace the ellipse. Third, place the second brad 3 inches (7.5 cm) away and use a green pen to draw the ellipse. **Science Fair Hint:** Title the series of drawings Shapes of Planetary Orbits. Label the drawings A, B, and C, with A being the most elongated ellipse and C the least. Prepare a legend, such as the one shown, indicating the focal distance of each orbit.

Legend	
Orbit	**Focal Distance, inches (cm)**
A	
B	
C	

SHOW TIME!

1. Using the focal distance of the orbit of each planet and the information from the previous experiment, prepare a listing of the planets' elliptical-shaped orbits in order from the least to the most elongated. The focal distance can be determined by subtracting a planet's minimum distance (M_2) from its maximum distance (M_1) from the Sun. (See the appendix for this information.)

   Use the equation below to calculate the focal distance of Earth, which would be F.

   $$F = M_1 - M_2$$

   where
   M_1 = 95 million miles (152 million km)
   M_2 = 92 million miles (147 million km)
   Example:
   F = 95 million miles (152 million km)
      − 92 million miles (147 million km)
      = 3 million miles (5 million km)

2. Pluto is generally the farthest planet from the Sun. However, during part of Neptune's orbit, Neptune is the farthest planet from the Sun. Use the maximum and minimum distances of Neptune and Pluto from the Sun to make a diagram to explain this phenomenon.

CHECK IT OUT!

Sir Isaac Newton (1642–1727), an English scientist, determined that planets stay in orbit because of the force of attraction between two bodies called *gravity*. Gravity also makes the planets move faster at the aphelion and slower at the perihelion of their orbit. For information about Newton's ideas about planetary movement, see pages 47–53 in David Filkin's *Stephen Hawking's Universe* (New York: Basic Books, 1997).

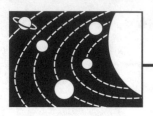

8

Twirlers

PROBLEM

How does the period of rotation of different parts of Earth compare?

Materials

one-hole paper punch
2 sheets of different colored paper
pen
paper plate
school glue
sharpened pencil
adult helper

Procedure

1. Use the paper punch to cut 6 circles from each color of paper.

2. Use the pen to mark a dot in the center of the plate. The plate represents Earth.

3. Glue the paper circles of one color around the edge of the plate and glue the other circles near the center of the plate. The paper circles represent different areas of Earth.

4. When the glue dries, ask an adult to insert the point of the pencil through the center of the plate so that the point exits through the dot.

5. Hold the pencil so that the side of the plate with the paper circles faces up. Rotate the pencil so that the plate turns

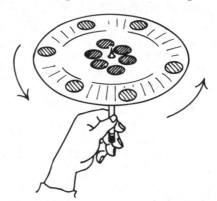

one full turn in a counterclockwise direction. Compare the movement of the paper circles on the edge of the plate with the movement of those in the center.

Results

The plate and all the paper circles move together, rotating in the same amount of time.

Why?

The paper plate, like the **terrestrial planets** (Earth-like planets that are small, dense, rocky worlds)—Mercury, Venus, Earth, and Mars—is solid, so all of its parts move together when it rotates. Therefore, the **period of rotation** (the time it takes for an object to make one complete rotation on its axis) is the same for all parts of Earth.

LET'S EXPLORE

Some celestial bodies, such as the Sun, Pluto, and the **Jovian planets** (Jupiter-like planets that are large, gaseous, low-density worlds)—Jupiter, Saturn, Uranus, and Neptune—are mostly spheres of gas. (Note that Pluto is gaseous but is not large like the Jovian planets, so it doesn't fit in either the terrestrial or Jovian category.) On Pluto and the Jovian planets, the period of rotation at the equator is different from that at the poles or points between. Demonstrate how different parts of a fluid can have different periods of rotation by replacing the paper plate with a small bowl of water. Drop one color of paper circles on the surface of the water around the bowl's edge and drop the other color of paper circles in the center of the bowl. Use your finger to stir the water in a counterclockwise direction. Compare the movement of the paper circles in the center with the movement of those on the outside. How do the periods of rotation of the two groups of paper circles compare?

SHOW TIME!

1. How do the periods of rotation of the other planets compare to that of Earth? Prepare a table similar to the one shown here, with the period of rotation of each of the nine planets in hours and in Earth days. (Use the periods of rotation of the planets in the appendix.) Since the period of rotation is given in hours, divide this by 24 to calculate Earth days. For example, Mercury's period of rotation is 1,407.5 hours. In Earth days, this would be 1,407.5 hours ÷ 24 hours = 58.6 Earth days.

Period of Rotation		
Planet	**Hours**	**Earth Days**
Mercury	1,407.5	58.6
Venus		
Earth		
Mars		
Jupiter		
Saturn		
Uranus		
Neptune		
Pluto		

2. How does the direction of rotation of the planets compare? All the planets and the Sun rotate in the same west-to-east direction as Earth, except for Venus and Uranus. Venus rotates in an east-to-west direction, and Uranus rotates east to west on its side. Model the direction of the rotation of Earth, Venus, and Uranus by following these steps to make three clay models:

- Shape a walnut-size piece of modeling clay into a ball.
- Insert a pencil representing the axis through the middle of the clay ball.
- Repeat these steps twice to make two more models.
- Use a pencil to label the three models E, V, and U.

Lay 2 index cards on a table. With the aid of two helpers, stand the models of Earth (E) and Venus (V) vertically on the cards. Tilt the Earth model (E) about 23° as shown. Hold the model for Uranus (U) sideways so that the eraser end (the north pole) is pointing toward the other models. As seen from the north pole of each model, turn Earth counterclockwise and Venus and Uranus clockwise. Use a photograph and/or diagrams of the models as part of your display to show the direction of rotation of these three planets.

CHECK IT OUT!

French physicist Jean-Bernard-Léon Foucault (1819–1868) used a pendulum made from a 223-foot (67-m) wire with a suspended sphere weighing 62 pounds (28 kg) to demonstrate that Earth rotates. Find out more about Foucault's pendulum. Where did Foucault perform his experiment? For information, see pages 25–30 in *Janice VanCleave's A+ Earth Science* (New York: Wiley, 1999).

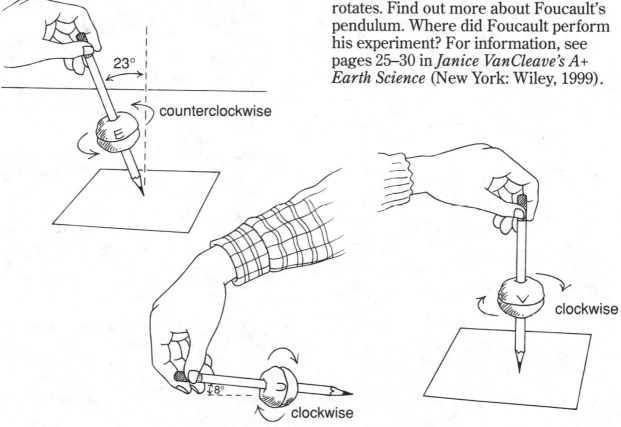

23°

counterclockwise

8°

clockwise

clockwise

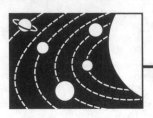

9

Brighter

PROBLEM

Why are planets and the Moon so bright in the sky?

Materials

transparent tape
sheet of typing paper
sheet of 9-by-12-inch (22.5-by-30 cm)
    white construction paper
medium-size box with one side at least
    9 by 12 inches (22.5 by 30 cm)
yardstick (meterstick)
3 or 4 books
flashlight

Procedure

1. Tape the typing paper to a wall so that its bottom edge rests on the floor. The paper represents the screen in a **photometer** (an instrument that measures the brightness of light) located at a point on Earth.

2. Tape the white construction paper to one side of the box. The paper represents the surface or atmosphere of a planet.

3. Stand the box 12 inches (30 cm) from the screen, with the paper-covered side of the box facing the screen.

4. Set the books near the wall to one side of the screen. Set the flashlight on top of the books so that its bulb is at an angle to the paper on the box and its light shines on the center of the construction paper.

5. Turn the flashlight on, then darken the room. Observe the brightness of the photometer screen.

6. Turn the flashlight off and again observe the brightness of the screen.

typing paper

9" × 12"
sheet of
construction paper

Results

The screen is bright only when the flashlight is on.

Why?

The Sun and other stars are **luminous** (giving off light). But the Moon and planets, even though they shine, are not luminous. These celestial bodies reflect (bounce back) light from the Sun to Earth, the same way the construction paper reflects the light from the flashlight to the screen. Without the Sun, the Moon and planets would not shine.

LET'S EXPLORE

1. Different planets and other celestial bodies, such as moons, reflect different

amounts of light. How does the color of a reflecting material affect the amount of light reflected? Repeat the experiment, placing the white construction paper on the box as before. Observe the brightness of the light reflected on the screen. Then, tape a different color paper, such as brown, over half of the white paper on the box. First shine the light on the white paper, then on the brown paper, and compare the brightness of the light reflected on the screen by each paper. Repeat using various colors, such as red, green, and black. From the results, determine how the surface or atmospheric color of a celestial body affects its brightness in the sky.

2. How does distance from the Sun affect a celestial body's **apparent brightness** (how bright a celestial body appears to be as observed from Earth)? Repeat the original experiment, placing the box at different distances from the screen. Place it at these distances: 6 inches (15 cm), 12 inches (30 cm), and 18 inches (45 cm). Adjust the angle of the flashlight at each distance so that its light strikes the center of the construction paper on the box

each time. Notice the screen's brightness at each distance. From the results, determine how distance from the Sun can affect a planet's apparent brightness. Can being too close to the Sun affect the visibility of a planet? For information, see chapter 15, "Blinding."

SHOW TIME!

1. The reflective power of a celestial body is called its **albedo,** which refers to the ratio of the amount of light received to the amount of light reflected from an object. (A **ratio** is a pair of numbers used in making a comparison. A ratio is a fraction. If the denomination is 1, such as 0.3/1, the number can be written as 0.3. An albedo of 1 indicates a shiny surface with a perfect reflection, while an albedo of 0.0 indicates a totally black surface with no reflection. Design a table comparing the albedos of the nine planets. One way is to list the planets in order from highest to lowest albedo. (See the appendix for the planets' albedos.)

2. Celestial bodies not only reflect light from the Sun, but can also reflect sunlight onto other celestial bodies.

Sunlight reflected off Earth onto the Moon is called **earthshine**. During the Moon's **crescent phase** (small, curved, lighted section), you can sometimes see the rest of the Moon's shape dimly lit as a result of earthshine.

To demonstrate the effect that earth-shine has on the appearance of the Moon, divide a lemon-size piece of dark-colored clay in half and roll the two parts into balls. Stick one ball on the end of a craft stick. This ball will represent the Moon. Use the other ball to stand the Moon model on a table. Use books to raise a flashlight so that its bulb is about 2 inches (5 cm) from the back side (the side away from you) of the clay Moon. In a darkened room, observe the darkness of the front side of the Moon model. Take a cotton ball and move it from side to side about 1 inch (2.5 cm) from the front side of the clay Moon. Observe the front side of the clay Moon as the cotton ball moves closer to it.

CHECK IT OUT!

Look at the Moon and you will see that some regions are darker than others. Early peoples imagined that these shadow areas were part of a human face, thus the saying "the man in the Moon." Find out more about the bright and dark features of the Moon. For information, see pages 6–9 in Fred Schaaf's *Seeing the Sky* (New York: Wiley, 1990).

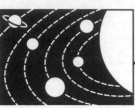

10

More or Less

PROBLEM

How do the masses of other planets compare to the mass of Earth?

Materials

pen
ruler
sheet of typing paper
calculator

Procedure

1. Use the pen, ruler, and paper to make a table like the one shown here.

2. Complete the table by calculating each planet's mass ratio, which is the ratio of a planet's mass to the mass of Earth. *NOTE: The mass of planets is measured in trillion trillion kg.* For example, the mass ratio of Mercury is:

mass ratio = planet's mass ÷ Earth's mass
= 0.33 ÷ 5.986
= 0.06/1

Mercury's mass ratio is 0.06/1, which means that Mercury's mass is 0.06 times that of Earth.

Mass Ratios of the Planets to Earth		
Planet	Mass (trillion trillion kg)	Mass Ratio (planet/Earth)
Mercury	0.33	0.06/1
Venus	4.87	
Earth	5.98	
Mars	0.64	
Jupiter	1,899.0	
Saturn	569.0	
Uranus	86.9	
Neptune	103.0	
Pluto	0.012	

Results

The mass ratio of each planet in the solar system is calculated.

Why?

The term mass ratio, as used in this book, is a number indicating how many times as massive as Earth a celestial body is. The mass ratio is calculated by dividing the mass of a planet by the mass of Earth.

LET'S EXPLORE

1a. A planet's **gravity** (the force of attraction between two bodies) increases with its mass. If only mass is considered, how would the gravity of planets compare to Earth's? Prepare a list of the planets' mass ratios in order, from greatest to least.

1b. The gravity multiple for planets is a number indicating how many times Earth's surface gravity another planet's surface gravity is. Make a list of the planets' gravity multiples in order from greatest to least. (For gravity multiples, see the Weight on Different Planets table in "Show Time!") How does this list compare with the list of mass ratios?

2. Surface gravity decreases as the diameter of a planet increases. Use the gravity multiples, mass, and the diameters of planets (see the appendix) to explain why:

- Venus and Uranus have about the same surface gravity
- Neptune has more surface gravity than Pluto

SHOW TIME!

Objects with a given mass would not weigh the same on other planets as on Earth. Make a table to compare your weight on Earth to what it would be on other planets. First, weigh yourself on a bathroom scale (weight on Earth). Then multiply your weight by the gravity multiple. For example, if you weigh 90 pounds (41 kg) on Earth, your weight on Mercury would be:

90 pounds (41 kg) × 0.38 = 34.2 pounds (15.58 kg)

Weight on Different Planets			
Planet	Weight on Earth, pounds (kg)	Gravity Multiple	Weight on Planet, pounds (kg)
Mercury		0.38	34.2 (15.58)
Venus		0.90	
Earth	90 (41)	1	90 (41)
Mars		0.38	
Jupiter		2.54	
Saturn		1.16	
Uranus		0.92	
Neptune		1.19	
Pluto		0.06	

CHECK IT OUT!

Earth's crust has a density of about 2.8 g/ml, while Earth as a whole has an average density of about 5.5 g/ml. (For comparison purposes, water has a density of 1 g/ml.) This indicates that the density of Earth's interior is greater than the density of the crust. Therefore, the interior must be made of denser material than the crust. What clues do the densities of other planets give to their composition? See the appendix in this book for the average density of each planet. For information, see pages 149–151 in Isaac Asimov's *Guide to Earth and Space* (New York: Fawcett Crest, 1991).

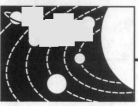

11

How Hot?

PROBLEM

How does a planet's distance from the Sun affect its temperature?

Materials

transparent tape
sheet of graph paper
ruler
flashlight
felt-tipped pen
helper

Procedure

1. Tape the graph paper to a wall at chest height.

2. Hold the end of the ruler perpendicular to the center of the graph paper.

3. Using the ruler as a guide, hold the flashlight ½ inch (1.25 cm) from the graph paper.

4. Shine the light on the paper and ask your helper to use the pen to trace around the circle of light.

5. Move the flashlight 2 inches (5 cm) from the paper and repeat step 4.

Result

The circle of light is larger when the light is farther from the paper.

Why?

Light from the flashlight spreads out just as light from most other sources does, including the Sun. Since the same amount of light left the flashlight regardless of the distance between the flashlight and the paper, the smaller circle of light indicates a more concentrated (gathered closely together) amount of light. Light is a form of energy. Thus, more energy was received in a smaller area when the flashlight was closer to the paper than when it was farther away.

Solar energy is energy from the Sun. Solar energy is a combination of different kinds of energy, including rays of visible and **infrared light** (rays that heat). The closer a planet is to the Sun, the more concentrated the solar energy it receives. The amount of solar energy a planet receives affects its surface temperature. The surface temperature of a planet decreases as its distance from the Sun increases, but other things affect surface temperature, such as the planet's atmosphere. See "Check It Out!" for more information about the effect of atmosphere on a planet's surface temperature.

LET'S EXPLORE

How does the way the axis of a planet is tilted in relation to the Sun affect their surface temperature? Repeat the experiment, attaching the graph paper to a clipboard and securing the flashlight to the ruler so that ½ inch (1.25 cm) of the ruler extends past the bulb end of the flashlight. Hold the ruler against the graph paper and ask your helper to make a drawing of the light. Then tilt the paper at an angle of about 45° from the light and ask your helper to make a second drawing of the light. What is the difference in the concentration of light between the two drawings? **Science Fair Hint:** Display the drawings to represent the results of the experiment.

SHOW TIME!

1. Any given area of a planet may not receive the same amount of light energy all year long. This is because the axes of planets are tilted in relation to their orbits around the Sun. The axis of Earth is tilted about 23°.

Demonstrate the effect that axial tilt has on the amount of solar energy Earth receives during the year.

Ask an adult to insert a pencil through a 3-inch (7.5-cm) Styrofoam ball. The pencil represents the axis. Place a rubber band around the center of the ball halfway between the top and bottom of the ball. This represents the equator. Hold the pencil vertically on a table with the eraser side up. In a darkened room, place a flashlight about 6 inches (15 cm) from the right side of the ball so that the center of the light falls on the rubber band. Tilt the top part of the ball to the right—toward the light. Observe how much light strikes the ball above and below the rubber band. Place the flashlight on the left side of the ball and keep the ball tilted to the right—away from the light. Observe how much light strikes the ball above and below the rubber band. Make a diagram showing the positions of the ball and the flashlight. Draw another diagram showing how the tilt of Earth's axis in relation to the Sun causes the seasons.

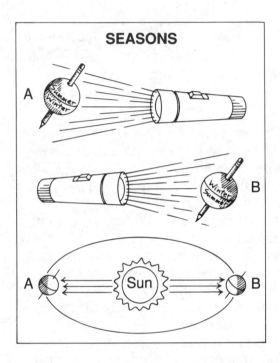

SEASONS

2. Because planets are spherical, surface areas on the daytime side of a planet are angled from the Sun by varying amounts from 0° to 90°. The areas of Earth that are not angled from the Sun at all are tilted at a 0° angle to the Sun's rays and receive the most concentrated light. Areas that are angled farthest from the Sun are tilted at a 90° angle to the Sun's rays and receive

the least concentrated light. At 0° surface tilt, the Sun's rays are perpendicular to the surface and at a 90° surface tilt, the Sun's rays are parallel to the surface. The diagram shows Earth on **spring equinox** (the first day of spring) and **autumn equinox** (first day of autumn). On these days, the equator has a 0° angle to the Sun's rays. Thus, it receives the most light, while the poles have a 90° tilt and receive the least amount of light. Design diagrams showing the degree of surface tilt at different areas of earth on the **summer solstice** (first day of summer) and **winter solstice** (first day of winter). For summer solstice, tilt Earth's north axis 23 degrees to the right. This tilts the equator on the Sun side of the drawing down 23 degrees. For the winter solstice, tilt the north axis 23 degrees to the left, so that the equator is tilted up 23 degrees. For more information about the surface tilt on these days, see pages 125–134 in *Janice VanCleave's Geography for Every Kid* (New York: Wiley, 1993).

ANGLES OF THE EARTH'S SURFACE TILT

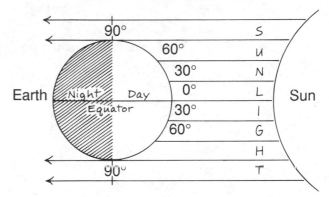

CHECK IT OUT!

The surface temperature of Mercury, the closest planet to the Sun, ranges from –279°F (–173°C) in the nighttime to 806°F (430°C) during the daytime. This planet has extremes of heat and cold because its atmosphere is so thin. Why is Venus, the second planet from the Sun, hotter than Mercury? Why is Earth's average temperature so moderate? Find out more about the surface temperature of each of the planets and how a planet's atmosphere or absence of it affects its temperature. For information, see Dinah L. Moche's *Astronomy Today* (New York: Random House, 1995).

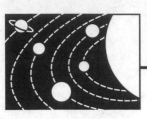

See-Through

PROBLEM

How does Mercury's atmosphere affect images of its surface?

Materials

red pen
ruler
drawing compass
two 3-by-5-inch (7.5-by-12.5-cm) white
   index cards
masking tape
flashlight
walnut-size piece of modeling clay
magnifying lens
two 9-ounce (270-ml) clear plastic
   glasses
helper

Procedure

1. Draw a red circle with a diameter of about ½ inch (1.25 cm) in the center of one of the index cards. Color in the circle.

2. Tape the index card to a wall just above a table so that the bottom of one long edge of the card rests on the table.

3. Turn on the flashlight and darken the room.

4. Lay the flashlight on the table at an angle to and about 4 inches (10 cm) from the index card. Position the flashlight, using clay as a support if necessary, so that its light shines on the red circle.

5. Holding the magnifying lens in one hand, position the lens opposite the flashlight at the same angle and distance from the index card on the wall.

Hold the second card in the other hand behind the lens and move both the lens and the card back and forth until the lens projects the best image of the red circle on the card.

6. With the lens and card in this position, ask your helper to set one of the empty glasses on the table between the flashlight and the red circle, and the second glass between the red circle and the magnifying lens. Observe any change in the appearance of the image of the red circle on the card.

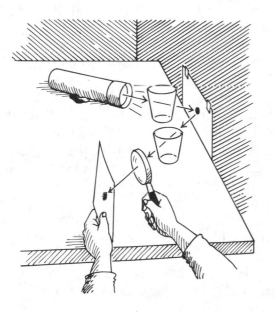

Results

The image of the red circle on the second index card was clearer before the glasses were set in place.

Why?

The red circle represents a location on the surface of Mercury. The flashlight is sunlight. The magnifying lens represents the lens of a camera used in spacecraft, and the second card is the photo (light)-sensitive electronic surface inside the camera, where the image is projected when a photograph is taken. The empty glasses represent the extremely thin atmosphere of Mercury, which contains helium, sodium, hydrogen, and possibly oxygen gases.

Part of the light reaching the red circle is absorbed by the paper and the rest is reflected away from the red circle. Some of this reflected light passes through the magnifying lens, and an image of the red circle is projected on the card in your hand. In the same way, light passes through a camera lens and is projected on the photo-sensitive surface inside the camera. If enough light from each part of the red circle is projected on the card, the image of the red circle will be bright and well defined.

The plastic glasses, like the atmosphere around Mercury, change the direction of light passing through them. Some of the light is reflected, some is refracted in different directions, and some passes straight through. Because of the change of the direction of the light, less light from the red circle passes through the lens, so the image of the red circle is not as clear and well defined as without the glasses. In a similar way, images of Mercury's surface are less clear because of its thin atmosphere.

LET'S EXPLORE

How does a thick atmosphere, like that around Venus, affect photographic or telescopic images of a planet's surface? Repeat the experiment. Once the glasses are in position and the image is projected on the card, make note of the brightness of the projected image as well as the brightness of the red circle drawn on the index card. Ask your helper to fill the glasses with water, then stir in 2 tablespoons (30 ml) of milk. The lack of clarity and definition of the red circle drawn on the card is an indication of how difficult it is to photograph the surface of Venus with its thick atmosphere. **Science Fair**

Hint: Ask your helper to take photos for a display to represent the procedure and results.

SHOW TIME!

The atmosphere of Venus is about 96 percent carbon dioxide, 3.5 percent nitrogen, and 0.5 percent water and acids. The thick clouds surrounding Venus are believed to be composed of sulfuric acid droplets and microscopic sulfur crystals. Venus's atmosphere is **opaque** (not allowing light to pass through). However, radio waves can easily pass through its atmosphere.

Demonstrate how scientists use radio waves to get a picture of Venus's surface. Use a ruler and pen to divide a 5-by-8-inch (12.5-by-20-cm) piece of white poster board into 1-by-½-inch (2.5-by-1.25-cm) rectangles, aligning the 1-inch (2.5-cm) side of the rectangles with the longest side of the poster board. Tape the back of the poster board to the long side of a shoe box. Inside the box, next to the side the poster board is taped to, make a landscape of mountains, valleys, and plains, using modeling clay and/or building blocks.

Tie an 8-inch (20-cm) piece of string around a weight, such as a washer. Use a

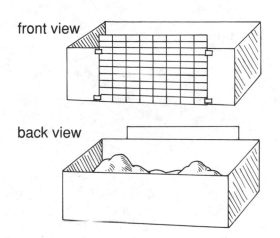

front view

back view

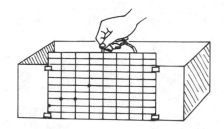

pen to mark off a ½-inch (1.25-cm) scale along the string. This string will be called the scale. Without looking behind the poster board, lower the scale at the top left corner until the weight touches something in the landscape. Use the marks on the scale to determine the height of the surface. Round off the measurement to the nearest scale marking, then make a dot on the left edge of the poster board at the point corresponding to the measurement on the scale. Repeat this procedure until a measurement has been made at each vertical line across the poster board. Then, use a pen to connect the dots. Label the poster board Radar Mapping and display it with your project.

In this experiment, the length of the string represents the time it takes for radio waves to reach a surface and bounce back. It takes less time for radio waves to reach a high surface, and more time to reach lower surfaces like valleys. Using this method, astronomers can tell what the landscape of a planet is like without ever seeing it.

CHECK IT OUT!

In 1989, the spacecraft *Voyager 2* flew within 3,125 miles (5,000 km) of Neptune. Thousands of images were sent back to Earth revealing that this planet has a very active atmosphere with a storm system as big as the whole Earth. Find out more about spacecraft views of the atmospheres of other planets. For information, see the different planets in Richard Moeschl's *Exploring the Sky* (Chicago: Chicago Review Press, 1993).

Big and Bigger

PROBLEM

How can the sizes of Mercury and Earth be compared?

Materials

12-by-12-inch (30-by-30-cm) piece of
  white poster board
drawing compass
metric ruler
scissors
pen

Procedure

1. On the poster board, draw a circle with a 3-cm diameter.

2. Cut out the circle and label it M for Mercury.

3. Cut another circle with an 8-cm diameter. Label the circle E for Earth.

4. Lay the circle representing Earth on a table. Determine how many Mercurys will fit across Earth's diameter by laying the Mercury model on the Earth model. Repeat steps 1 and 2 if more than one Mercury model is needed.

Results

The number of Mercurys that fit across Earth's diameter is about 2⅔.

Why?

The **equatorial diameter** (the distance through the center of a celestial body at its equator) of Earth is about 8,000 miles (12,800 km). Mercury's equatorial diameter is about 3,000 miles (4,800 km). Thus, Earth's diameter is about 2⅔ times bigger than Mercury's diameter. In this experiment, the Earth and Mercury models are made to a scale of 1 cm : 1,000 miles (1,600 km). The diameter of the Earth model is 2⅔ bigger than the diameter of the Mercury model.

LET'S EXPLORE

Compare the equatorial diameters of the other planets in our solar system to that of Earth by repeating the experiment, using the measurements in the Planets' Scaled Diameters table shown here. *NOTE: Large boxes or poster paper can be used instead of poster board to make the larger models.* **Science Fair Hint:** Use photos of the models as part of your display.

Planets' Scaled Diameters, 1 cm : 1,000 miles (1,600 km)	
Planet	Scaled Diameter (cm)
Mercury	3
Venus	7.5
Earth	8
Mars	4.2
Jupiter	90
Saturn	75
Uranus	32
Neptune	31
Pluto	1.4

SHOW TIME!

1a. The diameter of Earth's Moon is about 2,000 miles (3,200 km). Why does the Moon appear to be so small in the sky? Determine how distance affects the apparent size of an object by first measuring the diameter of an object, such as a wall clock. Then stand across the room from the clock. Holding a ruler at arm's length, close one eye and measure the apparent diameter of the clock. Compare the two measurements.

1b. Hold a ruler at arm's length as in the previous experiment to determine the apparent diameter of the full

moon. How does this measurement compare to the actual diameter of the Moon?

2. The diameter of the Sun is about 870,000 miles (1,390,000 km). Design a way to make a scale drawing of the Sun using the scale of 1 cm : 1,000 miles (1,600 km). One way would be to draw a circle in chalk on an empty parking lot or outdoor basketball court. Use a strong cord 440 cm long. Lay the cord on the ground. Tie one end of the cord around a piece of chalk. Have a helper hold the free end of the cord against the ground. Keeping the cord taut, use the chalk to draw a circle on the ground as your helper rotates with the end of the cord in the center of the circle. Since about 5 cm of the cord is used to attach the chalk, the circle has an approximate radius of 435 cm. Since a circle's radius is half of its diameter, the diameter of the circle is 870 cm. Display photos of the scale drawing of the Sun.

CHECK IT OUT!

The Moon's apparent size is larger when it is near the horizon than when it is high in the sky. This is an optical illusion. What causes this? For information and experiments to explain this illusion, see pages 15–17 in Fred Schaaf's *Seeing the Sky* (New York: Wiley, 1990).

14

Backward

PROBLEM

Why does Venus sometimes appear to stop moving as seen from Earth?

Materials

black marker
paper plate
2-yard (2-m) strip of adding machine
   paper
yardstick (meterstick)
transparent tape
2 pencils
grape-size ball of modeling clay
writing paper
helper

Procedure

1. Use the marker to draw a sun in the center of the plate.

2. Make two marks on the edge of the plate, one at the top and the other at the bottom. Label the top mark 1 and the bottom mark 2.

3. Place the paper strip on a table. With the marker, write E on the left end of the paper strip and W on the right end.

4. Starting 6 inches (15 cm) in from the right end of the paper, the end with the W, draw 11 large stars 6 inches (15 cm) apart. Number the stars, from 1 at the W end to 11 at the E end.

5. Use tape to secure the paper strip to the wall 1 yard (1 m) above and parallel to the floor.

6. Set a chair 2 yards (2 m) from the wall so that it faces the paper strip.

7. Insert the point of one of the pencils into the clay ball.

8. Sit in the chair and support the underside of the plate with your right hand at arm's length so that the plate is parallel

to the floor and mark 1 points toward the paper strip on the wall. Close one eye and position the plate so that mark 1 is centered slightly below star 6, the center star.

9. Hold the pencil in your left hand so that the ball hangs down. Adjust the distance between the plate and you until the lower edge of the ball can be held so that it almost touches the edge of the plate at mark 1.

10. Keeping one eye closed, slowly move the pencil so the clay ball moves in a counterclockwise direction near the edge of the plate from mark 1 to mark 2. As the ball moves, call out each of the star numbers on the paper strip that the clay ball passes

in front of. Ask your helper to record these numbers. Stop when the ball is in front of mark 2 on the plate.

11. Repeat step 10, moving the ball counterclockwise from mark 2 to mark 1.

Results

From mark 1 to 2, the sequence of the numbers increases, then the same number is repeated several times before the numbers get smaller. From mark 2 to 1, the reverse occurs. The numbers continue to get smaller, then the same number is repeated several times before the numbers increase.

Why?

The clay ball represents Venus, an **inferior planet** (a planet whose orbit is closer to the Sun than Earth's). The edge of the paper plate is the planet's orbital path, and your head is Earth. As Venus revolves in its orbit, as seen from Earth from night to night, the planet appears at times to move eastward in relationship to the stars, indicated by an increase in the recorded numbers. But then the planet seems to stop, indicated by the repeated star number, and then moves westward, indicated by the smaller numbers.

The apparent backward or westward motion of a planet such as Venus in relation to the stars as seen from Earth is called **retrograde motion.** As Venus moves around the back side of the Sun (the side of the plate away from you), it appears to move eastward. But as Venus moves toward Earth, it seems to stop. Then, when Venus passes Earth on the same side of the Sun (the side of the plate near you), it passes Earth and retrograde motion occurs: Venus appears to move westward. As Venus moves away from Earth, Venus again seems to stop for a time, then appears to move eastward around the back side of the Sun. Like Venus, Mercury is an inferior planet and is more difficult to see, but it is visible from Earth and has a similar retrograde motion.

LET'S EXPLORE

In the experiment, the Earth model (your head) was held stationary. But as Venus is viewed from Earth, both Venus and Earth are revolving around the Sun. Determine the effect of Earth's movement on Venus's apparent motion in relation to the background of stars. Do this by repeating steps 1 through 9. Holding the pencil and plate stationary, observe the stars behind the clay ball as you move your head slightly to the right. Note any apparent motion of the clay ball. Use this information to explain why, as seen from Earth, the path of the inferior planets in relationship to the stars appears to be toward the east. **Science Fair Hint:** Make drawings of the position of Earth, Venus, and the Sun when Venus appears to be (1) moving east, (2) moving west, and (3) stopped. Note on the diagrams where retrograde motion occurs.

SHOW TIME!

The **superior planets** (planets whose orbits are farther from the Sun than Earth's) exhibit retrograde motion, and the ones visible with the naked eye are Mars, Jupiter, and Saturn.

The superior planets appear to have retrograde motion because Earth makes one revolution around the Sun in less time than it takes these planets to do so. Thus, Earth speeds ahead of these planets, giving them the appearance of moving backward in relation to the stars. Demonstrate the apparent backward motion of the superior planets by asking a helper to stand about 4 feet (1.2 m) in front of you. Take a photo showing your helper's head and the background beyond. Ask your helper to start walking slowly forward. At the same time, walk in the same direction at a faster speed than your helper. Observe the background beyond your helper's head when you are in line with each other. Stop and take a photo showing your helper's head and the background. Continue to walk at a faster speed until you are about 4 feet (1.2 m) ahead of your helper. Stop again and take a third photo of your helper's head and the background. The sequence of photos will show that your helper's head appears to move backward against the background. Display the three photos to show retrograde motion.

CHECK IT OUT!

Retrograde comes from Latin words meaning to step backward. Using this definition of retrograde motion, why is Uranus's rotation technically considered retrograde motion? For information, see pages 131–132 in Ann-Jeanette Campbell's *Amazing Space* (New York: Wiley, 1997).

15

Blinding

PROBLEM

Why is it sometimes difficult to see an inferior planet?

Materials

scissors
drawing compass
ruler
black construction paper
white chalk
transparent tape
pencil
flashlight

Procedure

1. Cut a circle with a diameter of about 1 inch (2.5 cm) from the black paper.

2. Use the chalk to make an X near the edge of the paper circle.

3. Tape the paper to the end of the pencil.

4. Grasp the end of the pencil and turn it so that the side of the paper with the chalk mark faces you.

5. Lay the flashlight on the table so that the bulb end is at the table's edge.

6. Turn the flashlight on and darken the room.

7. Sit on the floor in front of the light so that you are facing the bulb. Hold the pencil at arm's length from your face and about 6 inches (15 cm) from the glowing bulb of the flashlight.

8. Observe the visibility of the chalk mark on the paper.

Results

When the paper is held in front of the light, the chalk mark cannot be seen.

Why?

This experiment demonstrates an inferior planet between Earth and the Sun, like the paper between you and the flashlight. The planet is only lit from behind, so the brightness of the Sun makes seeing the dark planet impossible. (Remember never to look directly at the Sun because it can permanently damage your eyes.) Only the inferior planets, Mercury and Venus, can move between Earth and the Sun.

LET'S EXPLORE

1. Venus and Mercury are best seen when they are as far east or west of the Sun as possible for observers on Earth. Repeat the experiment, but this time move the paper first about 4 inches (10 cm) to the left of the light, then about 4 inches (10 cm) to the right of the light. Then move the paper about 6 inches (15 cm) to either side of the light. In each position, note the visibility of the chalk mark.

2. Even when Venus and Mercury are far to the east or west of the Sun, it is more difficult to see them if the Sun and the planets both are above the horizon. Demonstrate this by repeating the previous experiment, holding the pencil with your left hand so that the paper circle is to the left of the bulb at the position where the chalk mark is most visible. Then hold an index card (the horizon) in your right hand about 6 inches (15 cm) from the bulb so that the card covers the blinding light of the bulb but allows you to see the chalk mark. Remove and replace the card several times to compare the visibility of the chalk mark with and without the blinding light of the bulb.

SHOW TIME!

1. The greater the angle between the Sun and an inferior planet as seen from Earth, the more visible the planet is. Diagram the positions of Venus where it is most visible from Earth. Use a drawing compass to draw a circle with a 1-inch (2.5-cm) diameter in the center of a 10-inch (25-cm)-square piece of white poster board. Around this circle draw two more circles, one with a diameter of 4 inches (10 cm) and the other with a diameter of 6 inches (15 cm). The larger circle

represents Earth's orbit, and the smaller represents the orbit of Venus. The innermost circle is the Sun. On the bottom of the Earth circle, trace around a penny to make a circle that represents the planet Earth. Lay a ruler across the centers of the Earth and Sun circles, and draw a straight line from Earth to the Sun. Tape an 8-inch (20-cm) piece of string to the center of the small circle. The straight line and the string are the arms of an angle. Holding the end of the string, stretch the string across the Venus circle. Where the string touches the circle is the position of Venus where it is most visible from Earth. Observe the size of the angle made by the line and the string. Move the string to find the other position on Venus's orbit where this angle is greatest. Mark an X at both positions.

2. If Venus is between the Sun and Earth, or if the Sun is between Earth and Venus, the Sun is too bright for us to see Venus. Find the sections on the orbit of Venus in the previous model where Venus cannot be seen from Earth, and use a colored pen to mark these sections. Make a legend for the model indicating that each X represents the most visible position of Venus, and the colored sections indicate where the planet cannot be seen.

CHECK IT OUT!

1. As viewed from Earth, Venus is the third brightest object after the Sun and the Moon. Find out more about the brightness of Venus. Why does it outshine most other celestial bodies?

For information, see page 106 in Ann-Jeanette Campbell's *Amazing Space* (New York: Wiley, 1997).

2. Mercury is so close to the Sun in the sky that it is generally difficult to ever see this planet. For a safe way of viewing Mercury, see page 65 in David H. Levy's *Skywatching* (San Francisco: Nature Company, 1995). This book also provides information about observing each of the other planets.

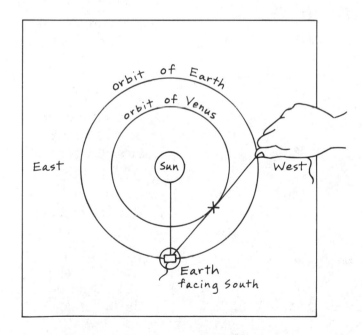

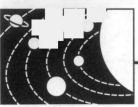

16

Ringed

PROBLEM

How do the rings of Saturn lie around the planet?

Materials

10-inch (25-cm)-square piece of white
   poster board
drawing compass
ruler
scissors
black marker or crayon
index card
walnut-size piece of modeling clay
wooden skewer
2-inch (5-cm) Styrofoam ball
transparent tape
protractor

Procedure

1. On the white poster board, use the compass and ruler to draw five circles, one inside the other, with these diameters: 2 inches (5 cm), 3 inches (7.5 cm), 7 inches (17.5 cm), 7½ inches (18.75 cm), and 8 inches (20 cm).

2. Working from the outside in, use the black marker to color between the second and third circles and between the fourth and fifth circles. The black areas represent space between the rings of Saturn.

3. Cut out the model of Saturn's rings by cutting around the outside of the largest circle. Then, cut away the center circle.

4. Lay the index card on a table and place the clay in its center.

5. Stick the wooden skewer through the center of the Styrofoam ball. Then place the paper rings model around the ball perpendicular to the skewer. Tape the underside of the rings to the skewer.

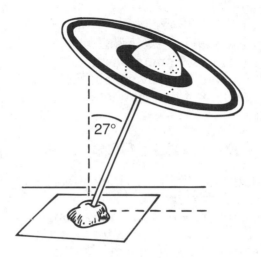

6. Stand the free end of the wooden skewer in the clay and tilt the rings toward you. Using the protractor, tilt the skewer about 27° to the index card.

Results

A model of Saturn is made showing two rings separated by a dark space.

Why?

The rings that you see around Saturn are actually thousands of separate ringlets made up of lots of small chunks of ice orbiting Saturn's equator. In 1656, Dutch astronomer Christiaan Huygens (1629–1695) announced that he observed a thin, flat, tilted disk around but not touching Saturn. In 1675, Giovanni Domenico Cassini (1625–1712), a French-Italian astronomer, observed that there was a dark space dividing the ring in two. This division—the outer black ring on your model—is called Cassini's division.

The model made in this experiment shows the two rings observed by Cassini divided by Cassini's division. Saturn's equator, and its rings, are always tilted at an angle of 27° to the plane of Saturn's orbit, represented by the index card in the experiment. Astronomers after Cassini found another division in the inner ring, dividing that ring into two more rings.

LET'S EXPLORE

How does the tilt of the rings affect their appearance from Earth? Demonstrate the appearance of the rings from Earth at different points in Saturn's orbit by positioning yourself at arm's length from the ball and at eye level with it. Close one eye and observe the rings with

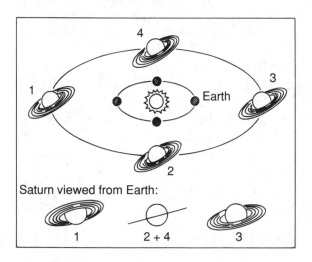

Saturn viewed from Earth:

your open eye. Watch the rings as you rotate the index card one full turn. Note how much of the rings is visible at different stages of the rotation.

SHOW TIME!

1. The rings of Saturn are always tilted at the same angle to Saturn's orbit, but they appear to spread out when viewed from the front and back and almost disappear when viewed edge on. From Earth, Saturn's rings appear to change size. This is because the rings are tilted relative to Earth's position, and as Saturn makes its 29-year orbit around the Sun, we see the rings from different points of view. Make a poster showing the positions of Saturn when the rings are widest and thinnest, such as the one shown here.

2. Saturn's rings are made up of chunks of ice. But because the distance from Earth to Saturn is so great, the rings appear solid to viewers on Earth. Demonstrate why this is so by using a paper punch to cut 30 to 40 circles from a sheet of white paper. In the center of a 4-inch (10-cm)-square piece of black construction paper, glue

the circles very close together in a
ring, like sprinkles on a doughnut.
Tape the black paper to a wall. Stand
near the paper and look at it, then
slowly back away until the circles look
like a solid ring.

CHECK IT OUT!

Saturn is now known to have seven
rings. The first three identified rings of
Saturn—A, B, and C—are visible with
small telescopes. What are the names,
order, and manner of discovery of the
other four rings? For information, see
pages 244–245 in Dinah L. Moche's
Astronomy (New York: Wiley, 1996).

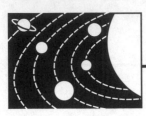

17

Space Rocks

PROBLEM

How can astronomers determine the shape of an asteroid?

Materials

transparent tape
sheet of typing paper
sheet of brown construction
  paper
pencil
flashlight

Procedure

1. Tape the typing paper to a wall at about shoulder height. This will be your screen.

2. Crumple the brown paper into a loose ball.

3. Tape the ball of brown paper to the pencil.

4. Darken the room and hold the flashlight in one hand to the side of the paper screen with its bulb pointing away from the screen. The screen and the flashlight should be at an angle of about 45°.

5. Holding the pencil in the other hand, position the brown paper ball in front of the flashlight so that light reflects off the ball and onto the screen. Adjust the angle of the flashlight if necessary.

6. Slowly rotate the pencil and observe the light reflected on the screen.

Results

The amount of light that is reflected changes as the paper ball rotates.

Why?

Asteroids are relatively small, irregularly shaped, rocky chunks of matter which rotate as they orbit the Sun. They are also called **minor planets.** In the experiment, the brown paper ball represents an asteroid, and the flashlight represents the Sun. The brightness of the light reflected off the paper ball fluctuates (changes continuously). Reflected sunlight bounces in a similar way from an asteroid to Earth. This is because aster-oids, like the paper ball, are irregularly shaped and rotate. Different parts of the asteroid reflect different amounts of light. Astronomers study the different amounts of light reflected by an asteroid to determine its shape.

LET'S EXPLORE

1. The amount of light reflected from an asteroid gives clues to its composition. About 95 percent of asteroids can be separated into two classes by composition, bright and dark. The bright asteroids are called **S-type asteroids** (stony) and the dark asteroids are called **C-type asteroids** (carbon). Repeat the experiment, using the brown paper ball to represent an S-type asteroid and a black paper ball to represent a C-type. Observe the difference in the light intensity of the two colors.

2. About 5 percent of asteroids have some metal composition and are called **M-type asteroids.** Prepare an M-type by repeating the experiment using a piece of aluminum foil. **Science Fair Hint:** Use clay as a stand for the three types of asteroids.

Fold an index card in half to make a stand-up label for each type. Use photographs of the asteroid models as part of your display.

SHOW TIME!

1. The largest asteroid, Ceres, has a diameter of about 600 miles (960 km). The state of Texas is about 740 miles (1,184 km) wide. Prepare a model to compare Ceres to the state of Texas. Cut out a road map of Texas and secure it to a piece of cardboard. Using the scale for the

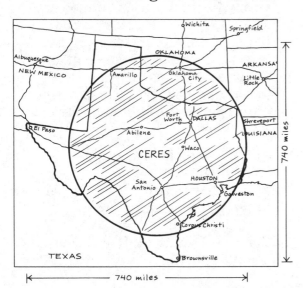

Texas map, cut out a tissue paper circle to represent Ceres. Secure the model of Ceres to the Texas map, making an effort to cover as much of the map as possible.

2a. Most asteroids orbit the Sun in a region called the **asteroid belt,** which lies between Mars and Jupiter. This belt is between 197 million miles (315 million km) and 309 million miles (495 million km) from the Sun. Design a 3-D model to represent the location of the asteroid belt. The model could be cardboard with loops of string glued on to represent the orbits. For planets and the Sun, attach different sizes of painted Styrofoam balls that have been cut in half by an adult. Gravel can be glued on to represent the asteroid belt. For information about why asteroids are in the belt, see page 24 in Sten Odenwald's *Astronomy Cafe* (New York: Freeman, 1998).

2b. Two groups of asteroids that do not lie in the asteroid belt, but move along the orbital path of Jupiter, are called **Trojan asteroids.** On Jupiter's orbital path, one of the

groups lies about 60° in front of Jupiter and the other lies about 60° behind it. Add the Trojan asteroids to the model made in the previous experiment.

CHECK IT OUT!

Not all asteroids are found beyond Mars. Some, such as the Apollo asteroids and the Aten asteroids, have orbits that cross Earth's. One theory of the extinction of dinosaurs is that a huge *meteorite,* which was all or part of an asteroid that crossed Earth's orbit, collided with Earth. Find out more about the effect of this collision. What evidence is there that a collision occurred? For information, see pages 113–114 in Isaac Asimov's *Guide to Earth and Space* (New York: Fawcett Crest, 1991).

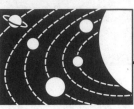

18

Dirty Snowballs

PROBLEM

What is a comet made of?

Materials

large white cotton ball
school glue
¼ teaspoon (1.25 ml) dirt (garden soil)

Procedure

1. Unroll the cotton ball and spread it into a square measuring about 3 by 3 inches (7.5 by 7.5 cm).

2. Pull a dime-size piece off one corner of the cotton square. Roll this piece into a ball.

3. Place 8 to 10 dots of glue on the rolled cotton, then sprinkle it with dirt.

4. Place the dirty cotton in the center of the cotton square. Wrap the cotton square around the dirty cotton to make a large ball about 1 inch (1.25 cm) in diameter.

5. Place 20 to 25 dots of glue on the cotton, then sprinkle it with dirt.

Results

A model of a comet's head is made.

Why?

A **comet** is a celestial body made of dust, gases, and ices (mainly water and carbon dioxide) that moves in an extremely elongated orbit about the Sun. The **head** of a comet is made of a **nucleus** (the central part of a material)

surrounded by a fuzzy starlike principal part called the **coma**. The nucleus may be only a few miles (km) in diameter and is made of ices, which are mainly water and carbon dioxide mixed with dust. The nucleus is described as a dirty snowball. In the model of a comet's head, the nucleus is the small, compact, dirty cotton ball surrounded by a coma, the large, fluffier, dirty cotton ball.

Far out in space, away from the Sun, the comet exists as only the nucleus, a dirty snowball. As the comet approaches the Sun, the ices **sublimate** (change from a solid to a gas without becoming a liquid), creating a cloud of dust and gas around the nucleus—the coma. A comet's head can have a diameter of 30,000 miles (48,000 km).

LET'S EXPLORE

When a comet is 2 AU from the Sun, solar wind blows some of the gas and dust away from the comet's coma. **Solar wind** is an energetic stream of particles constantly moving away from the Sun. The stream of gas and dust blown away from the coma generally divides, forming two comet tails. One of the tails, called an ion tail, is composed of gas that is **ionized** (electrically charged) by the solar wind. This ionized gas is blue in color and is lightweight enough to be swept in a line away from the Sun. The other tail, called a **dust tail,** is made of heavier solid dust particles separated from the coma as the comet orbits the Sun. The larger the dust particles, the less they are swept away from the curved orbital path. The shape of the dust tail is an indication of the size of the dust particles. The more curved it is, the larger the particles.

Complete the comet model by adding the two tails to the comet's head made in the previous experiment. Use blue and white paper, such as 2-inch (5-m)-wide crepe paper. Cut two 6-foot (1.8-m) strips of each color. Fold each strip of paper in half and cut along the fold to form four 1-inch (10-cm)-wide strips of each color. Glue the strips together at one end, first the blue strips, then the white strips on top. Glue the comet head to the glued end of the strips. Allow the glue to dry. This should take 15 to 30 minutes.

Ask an adult to tape the comet's head to the wall, at least 6 feet (1.8 m) from the floor. Allow the blue paper strips to hang straight down, but tape the white strips to the wall so that they curve to one side. The blue strips represent the ion tail, the white strips the dust tail.

SHOW TIME!

The scale of the comet model is 1 inch (2.5 cm) : 30,000 miles (48,000 km). Thus, the tails are 2.16 million miles (3.46 million km) long. Use a yardstick (meterstick) to mark off inches (cm) on a 2-inch-by-6 foot (5-cm-by-1.8-m) piece of adding machine tape. Secure this tape next to the comet model. Take a photograph of the model and display an enlarged copy of the photograph.

CHECK IT OUT!

Some comets are bright because of how close they are to Earth, such as Comet IRAS-Araki-Alcock, which passed 0.031 AU from Earth in May 1983. Other comets are bright because of their size, such as the Great Comet of 1811. Comet Halley was a spectacular sight in the sky in 1910. The apparent length of its tail on that occasion was the longest recorded for any comet. Why was

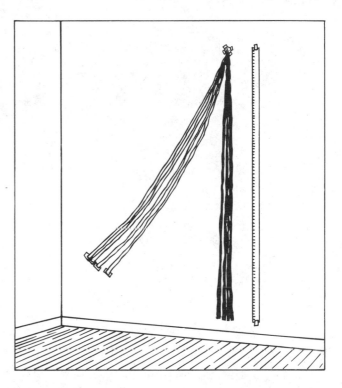

Halley's comet less spectacular in 1986? What things other than size and distance from Earth affect the brightness of comets? Find out more about what makes a comet "great." For information, see pages 39–47 in Alan Hale's *Everybody's Comet* (Silver City, NM: High-Lonesome Books, 1996).

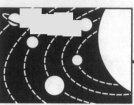

19

Shooting Stars

PROBLEM

Why are meteors hot?

Materials

bulb-type thermometer
writing paper
pencil

Procedure

1. Press the bulb of the thermometer between the palms of your hands. Record the temperature on the thermometer after 15 seconds or more. *CAUTION: Take care not to press so hard as to break the thermometer.*

2. Set the thermometer aside and rub the palms of your hands together as you count slowly to 10.

3. Immediately repeat step 1.

Results

The temperature reading increases after your hands are rubbed together.

Why?

Particles from comets, asteroids, or even moons and planets that float around in space are called **meteoroids**. Meteoroids from comets are generally very small, lightweight specks of dust, while meteoroids from other celestial bodies are generally larger and heavier. Most of the larger meteoroids come from asteroids.

When a meteoroid enters Earth's atmosphere, it is referred to as a **meteor.** Because it is moving so fast, the meteor is heated by **friction** (resistance of one body moving against another body) with air to a state of **incandescence** (glowing hot) and burns up. The particle as well as the glow it produces are both called a meteor. Most meteors are specks of comet dust. Large meteoroids create such brilliant meteors that they are called **fireballs.** The friction between your hands as you rub them together produces heat just as meteors do when they rub against air as they move through Earth's atmosphere.

LET'S EXPLORE

Meteoroids enter Earth's atmosphere at speeds of 22 to 60 miles (35 to 95 km)

per second. How does the speed of a meteoroid affect how much it is heated as it moves through Earth's atmosphere? Repeat the experiment, rubbing your hands together as quickly as possible.

SHOW TIME!

1a. Meteors appear as bright streaks of light across the sky. These flashes of light are commonly called **shooting stars**. On a dark, clear night, in an open area clear of trees or buildings, sit in a lawn chair so that you can observe the eastern sky. Record the time when you start your observations. Study the sky for 1 hour or more, counting the number of shooting stars you see. Record the time when you stop observing and determine the total number of hours of observation time. Calculate the average number of shooting stars per hour. For example, if during an observation time of 2 hours, 16 shooting stars are seen, the number of shooting stars per hour would be:

16 shooting stars ÷ 2 hours = 8 shooting stars per hour

1b. Are meteors seen more in the east than in the other compass directions: west, north, or south? Repeat the experiment with three friends. Have each person face one of the four compass directions. For best results, repeat the experiment on as many nights as possible. Average the results for each direction.

1c. Is the path of meteors generally random in direction, or do meteors come from a specific direction? While counting the meteors in the previous experiment, make note of the direction each meteor comes from. Use a star chart, similar to the one shown here, to plot the path of the meteors. A star with a tail can be the symbol of a meteor. Constellations can be added for reference. For charts of constellations visible in different seasons, see pages 224–227 in *Janice VanCleave's Constellations for Every Kid* (New York: Wiley, 1997).

2. As a comet orbits the Sun, it leaves behind a band of meteoroids that follow the comet's orbit. When Earth, moving along its orbit around the Sun, passes through the band of meteoroids, many meteors are seen coming from one part of the sky. This occurrence is called a **meteor shower.** Repeat the three previous

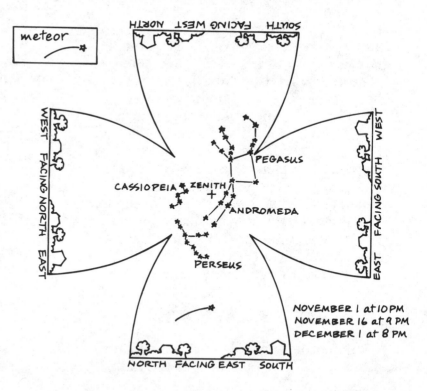

experiments during a meteor shower. Some of the dates for meteor showers are listed here. For a more detailed listing and more information about each of the showers, see page 96 in David H. Levy's *Skywatching* (San Francisco: Time Life/Nature Company, 1995).

Important Annual Meteor Showers

January	2–3	October	8–10
April	20–22	October	18–23
May	4–6	November	8–10
August	10–13	December	10–12

CHECK IT OUT!

Meteor showers are usually named for the constellation from which they seem to originate, such as Orionids from the direction of Orion. Find out more about meteor showers. What is a radiant? Why are meteors more plentiful after midnight? For information, see page 292 in Dinah L. Moche's *Astronomy* (New York: Wiley, 1996).

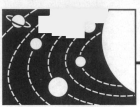

20

Splat!

PROBLEM

What happens when a meteorite strikes a planet?

Materials

1 cup (250 ml) sand or cornmeal
cereal bowl
flat toothpick
2 fine-point felt-tip pens—1 black, 1 red
walnut-size piece of modeling clay
ruler

Procedure

1. Pour the sand into the bowl, and shake the bowl so that the surface of the sand is as level as possible.

2. Insert the toothpick vertically in the center of the sand. The tip of the toothpick should touch the bottom of the bowl.

3. Use the black pen to mark a line on the toothpick level with the surface of the sand. Remove the toothpick and set it aside.

4. Shape the clay into a ball.

5. With one hand, hold the ruler vertically next to the bowl. With your other hand, hold the clay ball over the center of the bowl in line with the 6-inch (15-cm) mark on the ruler. Drop the ball.

6. Carefully remove the ball from the sand so that you disturb the sand as little as possible.

7. Insert the toothpick in the center of the hole in the sand made by the ball.

8. Use the red pen to mark a line on the toothpick level with the surface of the sand in the center of the hole. This mark should be on the same side of the toothpick as the first mark.

9. Measure the distance between the two marks on the toothpick to determine the depth of the hole.

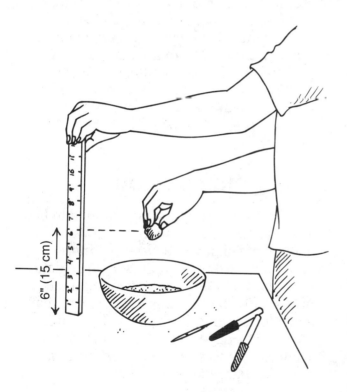

Results

The depth of the hole in the sand will vary depending on the size and weight of the clay ball. The author measured a hole ½ inch (1.25 cm) deep.

Why?

If a meteoroid does not burn up in Earth's atmosphere and strikes the ground, it is called a **meteorite**. Meteorites made of material similar to Earth's outer rock layer are called **stony meteorites.** This experiment demonstrates the results of the impact of a stony meteorite in soft sand. On impact, the sand is pushed out of the way, creating an **impact crater** (a bowl-shaped depression caused by the impact of a solid body).

Most meteorites range from a dust speck to larger ones that strike Earth with no more energy than a falling hailstone. But about 50,000 years ago, a meteorite as large as a house hit Earth with the energy of a nuclear weapon. The crater produced was ¾ mile (1.2 km) in diameter and 667 feet (200 m) deep. It is found in Arizona and is called the Barringer Meteorite Crater.

LET'S EXPLORE

1. How would the composition of the meteorite affect the results of its impact? **Iron meteorites** contain about 90 percent iron and are almost three times as heavy as stony meteorites. Demonstrate the difference in the impact of a heavier meteorite by repeating the experiment, using an equal size but heavier piece of clay. The weight can be increased by wrapping clay around 3 to 4 metal washers. Use a different color pen to mark the toothpick. Compare the depth of the impact craters of the two types of meteorites. **Science Fair Hint:** Photograph the sand before and after impact. Display the photos to represent the results.

2. How does the composition of the surface of a celestial body affect the type of impact crater formed? Repeat the original experiment, using flour instead of sand.

SHOW TIME!

Impact cratering is the process by which objects from space form craters on surfaces of celestial bodies the objects strike. This has occurred on every terrestrial planet and nearly every satellite in the solar system. Prepare a poster, such as the one shown here, depicting the four basic steps of impact cratering.

For information about each step and suggestions for figures, see page 86 in Heather Couper and Nigel Henbest's *How the Universe Works* (New York: Reader's Digest, 1994).

CHECK IT OUT!

Most meteorites are determined to be as old as the solar system itself, which is about 4.5 billion years. Find out more about meteorites. How do scientists date a meteorite? Are there any young meteorites? How can scientists determine that a meteorite came from Mars? For information, see pages 28–29 in Thomas R. Watters's *Planets: A Smithsonian Guide* (New York: Macmillan, 1995).

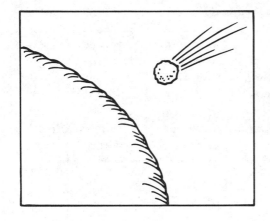

1.
Meteorite falling toward the surface

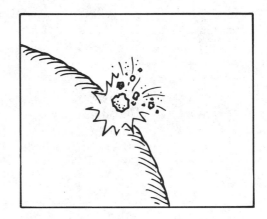

2.
Impact

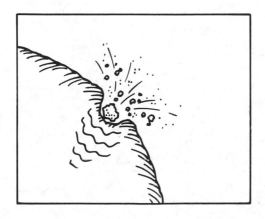

3.
Shock waves

4.
Explosion

Appendix

Planet Facts and Figures

Celestial Body	Equatorial Diameter, miles (km)	Average Density, g/ml (water = 1)	Albedo	Maximum Distance from Sun, millions of miles (millions of km)	Minimum Distance from Sun, millions of miles (millions of km)	Average Distance from Sun, millions of miles (millions of km)	Period of Rotation, hours
Mercury	3,048 (4,878)	5.4	0.1	44 (70)	29 (46)	36 (58)	1,407.5
Venus	7,562 (12,100)	5.2	0.76	68 (109)	67 (107)	68 (108)	5,832
Earth	7,973 (12,756)	5.5	0.39	95 (152)	92 (147)	94 (150)	24
Mars	4,247 (6,796)	3.9	0.16	156 (249)	129 (207)	143 (228)	24.6
Jupiter	89,875 (143,800)	1.3	0.51	510 (816)	463 (741)	486 (778)	9.8
Saturn	75,412 (120,660)	0.7	0.61	942 (1,507)	842 (1,347)	892 (1,427)	10.2
Uranus	31,949 (51,118)	1.2	0.35	1,875 (3,000)	1,712 (2,740)	1,794 (2,870)	17.2
Neptune	30,937 (49,500)	1.7	0.35	2,838 (4,540)	2,782 (4,452)	2,810 (4,496)	16
Pluto	1,434 (2,294)	1.8	0.5	4,604 (7,366)	2,771 (4,434)	3,688 (5,900)	153.4

Glossary

albedo   The ratio of the amount of light received to the amount of light reflected from an object.

annular eclipse   A solar eclipse in which none of the umbra of the Moon's shadow reaches Earth, the Moon appears smaller than the Sun, and an outer ring of the Sun's photosphere is visible.

aphelion   The point farthest from the Sun on the orbit of a celestial body.

apparent brightness   How bright a celestial body appears to be as observed from Earth.

asteroid belt   The region between Mars and Jupiter where most asteroids orbit the Sun.

asteroids   Relatively small, irregularly shaped, rocky chunks of matter which rotate as they orbit the Sun. Also called **minor planets.**

astronomer   A scientist who studies the stars and other celestial bodies.

astronomical unit (AU)   93 million miles (149 million km), the average distance between Earth and the Sun.

atmosphere   The blanket of gas surrounding a celestial body.

autumn equinox   The first day of autumn.

axis   An imaginary north-to-south line through the center of a celestial body.

celestial bodies   Natural objects in the sky, such as stars, suns, moons, and planets.

celestial equator   The equator of the celestial sphere, which is an extention of the Earth's equator.

celestial globe   A model of the celestial sphere.

celestial sphere   The imaginary sphere that has Earth at its center and all other celestial bodies stuck to its inside surface.

circumpolar stars   Stars that stay above the horizon.

coma   The principal part of a comet, made of a large gas and dust layer that surrounds the nucleus of a comet.

comet   A celestial body made of dust, gases, and ices (mainly water and carbon dioxide) that moves in an extremely elongated orbit about the Sun.

constellations   Groups of stars that appear to make patterns in the sky.

crescent phase   The Moon phase in which only a small, curved section of the Moon is lighted.

C-type asteroid   A carbon asteroid.

density   A measure of the amount of mass in a specific volume.

dust tail   One of two tails of a comet, composed of solid dust particles.

earthshine   Sunlight reflected off Earth that dimly lights the dark part of the Moon during different partially lighted phases.

eclipse   A celestial event that occurs when one celestial body passes in front of and covers another. To pass in front of and cover.

ellipse   An oval shape, which has two foci.

equator   An imaginary circle that divides a celestial body or celestial sphere in half.

equatorial diameter   The distance through the center of a celestial body at its equator.

fireballs   Large, brilliant meteors.

first quarter moon   The Moon phase following new moon, in which half of the side of the Moon facing Earth is lighted.

fluid   A gas or liquid.

focal distance   The distance between foci.

foci (singular **focus**)   Points in line and on either side of the center point of an ellipse.

frequency   The number of vibrations in a specific time period.

friction   The resistance of one body moving against another body.

full moon   The Moon phase in which Earth is between the Moon and the Sun. The side of the Moon facing Earth is fully lighted.

geocentric   Earth-centered.

gravity   The force of attraction between two bodies; the pull of objects near or at Earth's surface toward the center of Earth.

head   The coma and nucleus of a comet.

heliocentric   Sun-centered.

helioseismology   The study of the interior of the Sun by observation of the Sun's vibrations.

horizon   An imaginary line where the sky seems to meet Earth.

impact crater   A bowl-shaped depression caused by the impact of a solid body.

impact cratering   The process by which objects from space form craters on surfaces of the celestial bodies the objects strike.

incandescence   A state of glowing hot.

inferior planets   Planets whose orbits are closer to the Sun than Earth's—Mercury and Venus.

infrared light   Rays that heat objects.

ionized   Electrically charged.

ion tail   One of two tails of a comet, composed of ionized gas.

iron meteorite   A meteorite that contains about 90 percent iron.

Jovian planets   Jupiter-like planets that are large, gaseous, low-density worlds—Jupiter, Saturn, Uranus, and Neptune.

luminous   Giving off light.

lunar eclipse   An eclipse in which Earth passes directly between the Sun and the Moon, so that the Moon passes into Earth's shadow.

mass   The amount of matter in an object.

meteor   A meteoroid, or the glow produced by a meteoroid when it enters Earth's atmosphere, is heated to a state of incandescence, and burns up.

meteorite   A meteoroid that does not burn up when it enters Earth's atmosphere, but strikes the ground.

meteoroids   Particles from comets, asteroids, and other celestial bodies that float around in space.

meteor shower   Many meteors seen coming from one part of the sky as Earth's orbit crosses the orbit of a band of meteoroids left behind by a comet.

minor planets   See **asteroids.**

Moon phases   See **phases of the Moon.**

moonrise   The time of day when the Moon rises above the eastern horizon.

moonset   The time of day when the Moon sets or sinks below the western horizon.

M-type asteroid   A metal asteroid.

new moon   The moon phase in which the Moon is between Earth and the Sun. Thus, the side facing Earth is dark.

northern hemisphere   The half of the celestial sphere above or north of the celestial equator. (Capitalized: the region north of Earth's equator.)

north pole   The northernmost point of a celestial body. (Capitalized: the northernmost point of Earth.)

nucleus   The central part of a material.

opaque   Not allowing light to pass through.

orbit   The curved path of one body around another. To move in such a path.

partial lunar eclipse   A lunar eclipse in which only part of the Moon passes into Earth's shadow.

partial solar eclipse   A solar eclipse that is visible to observers in the penumbra of the Moon's shadow, so that only part of the Sun is blocked by the Moon.

penumbra   The lighter outer region of a shadow.

perihelion   The point closest to the Sun on the orbit of a celestial body.

period of rotation   The time it takes an object to make one complete rotation on its axis.

phases of the Moon   As seen from Earth, the changes of the Moon's shape during the month. Also called **Moon phases.**

photometer   An instrument that measures the brightness of light.

photosphere   The bright visible surface of the Sun.

planet   (from the Greek word meaning to wander) A celestial body that orbits a sun and shines only by the light it reflects.

Polaris   The North Star, the star closest to the point above Earth's North Pole.

ratio   A pair of numbers used in making a comparison; can be written as a fraction or its equivalent.

reflect   To bounce back, as light off an object.

refract   To bend light.

retrograde motion   The apparent backward or westward motion of a planet in relation to the stars as seen from Earth.

revolve   To move around a center point, as planets revolve around a sun.

rotate   To turn on an axis.

satellite   A body revolving around another body, such as the Moon around Earth.

scale model   A model made in proportion to the object or objects that it represents.

shooting star   The common name for **meteor.**

solar eclipse   An eclipse in which the Moon passes directly between the Sun and Earth, covering the Sun.

solar energy   Energy from the Sun.

solar system   A group of celestial bodies that orbits a star called a sun.

solar wind   An energetic stream of particles constantly moving away from the Sun.

south pole   The southernmost point of a celestial body. (Capitalized: the southernmost point of Earth.)

spectrum   A band of colored lights produced when visible light is separated.

spring equinox   The first day of spring.

stony meteorite   A meteorite made of material similar to the Earth's outer rock layer.

S-type asteroid   A stony asteroid.

sublimate   To change from a solid to a gas without becoming a liquid.

summer solstice   The first day of summer.

sun   A star that is the celestial body at the center of a solar system. (Capitalized) The central body in our solar system.

sunspots   Cool, dark spots on the Sun's surface.

superior planets   Planets whose orbits are farther from the Sun than Earth—Mars, Jupiter, Saturn, Uranus, Neptune, and Pluto.

terrestrial planets   Earth-like planets that are small, dense, rocky worlds—Mercury, Venus, Earth, and Mars.

third quarter moon   The Moon phase following full moon, in which half of the side of the Moon facing Earth is lighted.

total lunar eclipse   A lunar eclipse in which all of the Moon passes into Earth's shadow.

total solar eclipse   A solar eclipse that is visible to observers in the umbra of the Moon's shadow.

Trojan asteroids   Asteroids that orbit along the orbital path of Jupiter.

umbra   The darker inner region of a shadow.

universe   All celestial bodies in space.

vibrate   To move quickly back and forth.

vibration   One back-and-forth motion of a vibrating object.

volume   The amount of space occupied by an object.

white light   Visible light made of different colors of light.

winter solstice   The first day of winter.

Index

granules, 15
gravity:
  definition of, 31, 41, 86
  effect of diameter on, 42
  effect of mass on, 41
  gravity multiples, 41, 42
heliocentric:
  Copernicus's ideas, 5, 8
  definition of, 5, 86
  Galileo's ideas, 8
helioseismology:
  definition of, 13, 86
  experiments, 12–13
horizon:
  definition of, 11, 86
  model of, 11
Huygens, Christiaan, 65
impact crater, 81, 86
impact cratering:
  definition of, 82, 86
  model of, 83
incandescence, 77, 86
inferior planets:
  definition of, 57, 86
  retrograde motion of, 56–59
  visibility of, 60–63
ionized, 74, 86
ion tail:
  definition of, 74, 86
  formation of, 74
  model of, 74–75
iron meteorite, 82, 86
Jovian planets:
  definition of, 33, 86
  period of rotation, 33
Jupiter:
  model of, 5
latitude, 11
light:
  sun, 44–47
  visible, 26
longitude, 11
luminous, 37, 86
lunar eclipse:

definition of, 25, 86
models of, 24–27
moon's color during, 26–27
partial, 25, 86
total, 24–25, 26–27, 87
Mars:
  model of, 5
  period of rotation, 32–35
mass:
  definition of, 13, 86
  of planets, 40–43, 84
mass ratio:
  calculations of, 40, 41
  definition of, 40, 41
Mercury:
  atmosphere, 47, 48–50
  distance from the Sun, 6, 84
  equatorial diameter, 52
  model, 5
  period of rotation, 32–34
  size of, 52–53
  surface temperature, 47
  visibility of, 60–63
meteor:
  definition of, 77–86
  modeling of, 76–77
  origin of, 77–78
  shower of, 78–79
meteorite:
  definition of, 71, 81, 86
  impact of, 80–83
  impact crater, 80–81
  iron, 82, 86
  stony, 81, 87
meteoroids:
  definition of, 77, 86
  origin, 77
  speed of, 77
meteor shower:
  definition of, 78, 86
  list of, 79
  origin of, 79

minor planet, see asteroids
Moon:
  apparent size, 20–23, 54, 55
  color of, 26–27
  crescent phase, 39, 85
  diameter, 20, 54, 55
  eclipse, 24–27, 86
  first quarter moon, 16, 18, 85
  full moon, 16, 18, 85
  light from, 36–37
  model of, 5, 18, 19
  moonrise, 16, 85
  moonset, 16, 85
  new moon, 18, 86
  orbit of, 21
  phases of, 16–19, 87
  size of, 20–23
  solar eclipse, 20–23, 87
  surface features, 18–19
  third quarter moon, 16, 18, 87
  waning of, 19
  waxing of, 19
moonrise:
  definition of, 16, 85
  timetable, 16
moonset:
  definition of, 16, 85
  timetable, 16
Neptune:
  orbit, 31
  period of rotation, 33–34
new moon:
  definition of, 18, 86
  model of, 18
  rising of, 16
  setting of, 16
Newton, Sir Isaac, 31
Northern Hemisphere:
  definition of, 9, 86
  model of, 9–10
North Pole, 11

definition of, 8, 9, 86
model of, 8–9, 11
nucleus:
  comet, 72–74
  definition of, 72, 86
opaque, 50, 86
orbit:
  aphelion, 30, 85
  definition of, 6, 86
  foci of, 28–31
  Neptune's, 31
  perihelion, 30, 86
  planet, 28–31
  Pluto's, 31
  shape, 28–31
partial lunar eclipse:
  definition of, 25, 86
  model of, 25
partial solar eclipse:
  definition of, 22, 86
penumbra:
  definition of, 22, 86
  model of, 22
perihelion:
  definition of, 30, 86
  model of, 30
period of rotation:
  definition of, 33, 87
  of Jovian planets, 33
  models of, 32–35
phases of the Moon:
  crescent, 39, 85
  definition of, 17, 87
  first quarter, 16, 18, 85
  full moon, 16, 18, 85
  new moon, 16, 18, 86
  observation of, 16–19
  table of, 16
  third quarter, 16, 87
photometer:
  definition of, 36, 87
photosphere, 22, 87
planets:
  albedo, 36–39, 84
  apparent brightness, 38